Who's Who in Shakespeare

By the same Author

OPERAMANIA
THEATREMANIA
THE WIT OF THE THEATRE

Who's Who in Shakespeare

ROBIN MAY

WITH A FOREWORD BY
JUDI DENCH

TAPLINGER PUBLISHING COMPANY
NEW YORK

First published in the United States in 1973 by
TAPLINGER PUBLISHING CO., INC.
New York, New York

Library of Congress Catalog Card Number: 73-5334

ISBN 0-8008-8269-5

Contents

Introduction

This biographical dictionary contains all Shakespeare's characters except for some of the smallest fry. Cross references, so necessary when many of them are referred to by more than one name, have been kept within bounds. For instance, though ROBIN GOODFELLOW passes the reader back to PUCK, POMPEY BUM is not also entered as BUM. Noble families are placed together wherever possible, as are friars. In such a work the logical position for an entry is not always the best.

It would be churlish not to acknowledge the moral support that two books in particular have given the author, namely F. E. Halliday's *A Shakespeare Companion*, and that huge American treasure trove of Shakespeareana, Campbell and Quinn's *The Reader's Encyclopedia of Shakespeare*. Comparisons between Shakespeare's historical characters and their actual counterparts have been kept to a minimum for reasons of space, but the interested reader can consult W. H. Thomson's *Shakespeare's Characters: A Historical Dictionary*. The final responsibility for deciding such weighty matters as which doctor is which in *Macbeth* rests, of course, with the author.

ROBIN MAY
Wimbledon, 1972

Foreword

What a good idea this book is! When I was reading it I wondered why on earth nobody had written one like it before. It really is a marvellous reference book and I do congratulate Robin May. Judging it simply from the actor's point of view, when you are asked to play a part in Shakespeare the very first thing you want to do is quickly turn up a book that says, for instance, this is the person who comes on at the end with that marvellous news! So I think that this book, miraculously concise, will certainly be the actor's friend. But not only that, it will be a book for students, ~nd one that can be picked up like an encyclopedia or a dictionary—but very much more entertaining.

I was amazed to find that there are so many named characters. Most people have their favourite and unfavourite ones. I haven't an actual favourite, but I enormously enjoyed doubling Hermione and her daughter Perdita in *The Winter's Tale*. I loved playing Juliet, and have always liked being in *Twelfth Night* and the *Dream*. I haven't much enjoyed *The Merchant of Venice* and couldn't get under the skin of Portia, though I had every help. In fact, I wouldn't like to meet any of the characters in the *Merchant*. And there are several characters in *King Lear* I would hate to meet! But I would have liked to meet Malvolio. I don't think Robin May is quite fair to him; one could have made a friend of him. I know he thinks himself above his station, but I feel that he's rather hard done by. There's something very dear about him, and he's quick to forgive, too.

Had I been a man I'd certainly have liked the opportunity

of playing the Fool in *Lear*, and Achilles in *Troilus and Cressida*—what marvellous parts! And perhaps Ariel. I know that Ariel is sometimes played by a woman, but I never feel that is right. As a young man I'd have wanted to play Ariel and Osric, and definitely Mercutio, but perhaps none of the very large tragic roles.

Some people say that Shakespeare's female parts are less good than they might be because he had to write them for boys. I don't agree at all. One of the many reasons that I love Shakespeare is that he wrote cracking good parts for women—marvellous parts—and very three-dimensional ones, never cardboard creations. I'm sure that one of the reasons that the plays have lasted is because directors and actors have had different thoughts about the characters and have brought out different aspects of them. Shakespeare certainly seems to have understood women as well as men, and he wrote about every sort of man and every sort of woman.

This book's stress on the small parts will make it so useful. For instance, who could expect a Third Gentleman to be a good part? Yet the 3rd Gent. in *The Winter's Tale* has a wonderful speech about the off-stage reunion of Leontes and Perdita. Shakespeare gives it to a minor character and it is a scene-stealer.

And now, on to the characters, great and small. . . .

JUDI DENCH

A

AARON: The spectacularly evil Moorish lover of Queen Tamora of the Goths. Amongst his coups are the murder of Bassianus by her sons and the execution of Titus' sons, Quintus and Martius, for the crime. He also persuades Titus that, if his hand is cut off, it will serve as ransom for his sons, and obligingly severs it for him, knowing that the two are doomed anyway. For his misdeeds he is buried 'breast-deep in earth' and then starved to death, lamenting only that he cannot perform other deeds, 'ten thousand worse than every yet I did'. He has a redeeming feature in his love for his and Tamora's black baby. *Titus Andronicus*

ABERGAVENNY, LORD: Arrested for treason. *Henry VIII*

ABHORSON: An aptly-named executioner who objects on principle to Pompey the Bawd helping him execute Barnardine, because 'he will discredit our mystery'. However, after being reprimanded by the Provost, he takes on Pompey as his assistant. *Measure for Measure*

ABRAHAM: A servant of Montague, who fights with the Capulets at the beginning of the play. *Romeo and Juliet*

ACHILLES: One of the Greek commanders, but by no means the heroic figure of Homer's 'Iliad'. In the play, he is committed as a Greek to fighting the Trojans, but is also, because of his love for Hector's sister, Polyxena, committed to cease fighting. The wily Ulysses is forced to remind him of his duty. What eventually stops him sulking in his tent is the death of his beloved friend, Patroclus, but Shakespeare does not follow Homer in the ensuing fight with

I

Hector. Instead of a heroic episode, Achilles orders his followers to murder the Trojan when he is unarmed. *Troilus and Cressida*

ADAM: An old retainer of the de Boys family. He tells Orlando that his brother plans to kill him, warns him that he must flee, and offers him all his savings of a lifetime. Then he goes with Orlando into exile, at which point the 'good old man' fades from the play. Shakespeare is supposed to have played the part. *As You Like It*

ADRIAN: A lord who attends Alonso, King of Naples, and is shipwrecked with him. He finds that the island's air 'breathes upon us here most sweetly'. *The Tempest*

ADRIANA: The wife of Antipholus of Ephesus and a scold. She jealously pursues the wrong Antipholus—of Syracuse— to an abbey, thinking he is her husband. There, an abbess tells her she is to blame for her husband's madness. When all the errors are sorted out, she and her husband are reconciled. *The Comedy of Errors*

AEGEON: A Syracuse merchant who is condemned to death for daring to land at Ephesus while searching for his son, one of the Antipholus twins, Ephesus and Syracuse being at loggerheads. All ends happily when he is reunited with his sons and his wife, Aemilia, and is pardoned by the ruler of Ephesus. *The Comedy of Errors*

AEMILIA: The wife of Aegeon. Thinking that her husband and two sons, the Antipholus twins, are dead, she becomes the Abbess at Ephesus. Without realizing it, she grants sanctuary to Antipholus of Syracuse, then sees Aegeon on his way to be executed. Finally, the family is reunited. *The Comedy of Errors*

AEMILIUS: A Roman noble who tells the Emperor that the Goths, led by Lucius, son of Titus, are advancing on Rome. He conveys the Emperor's wish for a parley to Lucius, and, later, is the first to hail Lucius as the new Emperor. *Titus Andronicus*

AENEAS: A Trojan general. He carries a challenge from Hector to the Greeks, and later tells his friend, Troilus, that he must give up Cressida to Diomedes. *Troilus and Cressida*

AGAMEMNON: The leading Greek commander at Troy. Often on stage, this 'great commander', as Ulysses calls him, has little part to play in the action. He resents the behaviour of Achilles and agrees to exchange Antenor for Cressida. *Troilus and Cressida*

AGRIPPA: Octavius Caesar's friend who suggests that Antony should marry Octavia, the sister of Octavius. He appears in a number of scenes with Octavius. *Antony and Cleopatra*

AGUECHEEK, SIR ANDREW: A foolish knight who is the suitor of Olivia, and whose hair hangs down 'like flax on a distaff'. He fears that being a 'great eater of beef' may have damaged his wits. Sir Toby Belch jokingly suggests that Sir Andrew should challenge the boy Cesario (Viola in disguise), then pretends that the youth is a fire-eater. Poor Sir Andrew is terrified by the ensuing and abortive combat, and is soundly beaten about the head by Viola's twin brother, Sebastian. He still seems to enjoy the company of the teasing Sir Toby, just as audiences always enjoy any competent actor as Sir Andrew. *Twelfth Night*

AJAX: A Greek commander, who is a far cry from Homer's heroic figure. In the play, Alexander describes him as 'churlish as the bear' and 'slow as the elephant'. Thersites calls him 'a mongrel beef-witted lord'. In modern parlance, he is muscle-bound, mentally and physically. Ulysses uses him to make Achilles jealous and sting him into action by having Ajax fight Hector. *Troilus and Cressida*

ALARBUS: The eldest son of Queen Tamora of the Goths. He is sacrificed by the sons of Titus to appease the spirits of their brothers, slain in the Gothic wars. *Titus Andronicus*

3

ALBANY, DUKE OF: The husband of Goneril. He comes to regard her as a fiend because of her gross behaviour towards her father, while she regards him as a 'milk-liver'd man'. However, he feels obliged to repulse the French troops brought to help the King by Cordelia. When Lear dies, Albany becomes King himself. *King Lear*

ALCIBIADES: An Athenian general who asks for a friend to be pardoned by the Senate but is refused. His anger causes his banishment. Timon gives him gold to help him attack Athens, which he conquers and then revenges himself on his and Timon's enemies. *Timon of Athens*

ALENCON, JOHN, DUKE OF: He supports the French Dauphin and admires Joan of Arc. He comments to the Dauphin that the famished English 'want their porridge and their fat bull beeves' and admiringly comments on the courage of such 'lean raw-boned rascals'. He reluctantly swears fealty to the English crown at the end. *1 Henry VI*

ALEXANDER: Cressida's servant, who gives her a very unflattering description of the thick-witted, stolid Ajax. *Troilus and Cressida*

ALEXAS: One of Cleopatra's attendants. His betrayal of Antony and subsequent hanging by Caesar is related by Enobarbus. *Antony and Cleopatra*

ALICE: One of Katharine of France's ladies. She gives Katharine an English lesson. *Henry V*

ALIENA: Celia's assumed name. *As You Like It*

ALONSO: The King of Naples, brother of Sebastian and father of Ferdinand. He has helped Antonio to drive Prospero from Milan, but is smitten by remorse and thinks of suicide when he believes his son is dead. He repents and finally restores Prospero's dukedom, then joyfully finds Ferdinand alive and betrothed to Miranda. *The Tempest*

AMBASSADORS FROM FRANCE: They present tennis balls as a gift from the Dauphin to the King, who is not amused at the implied insult to his character. *Henry V*

AMIENS: One of the followers of the banished Duke in Arden. He sings 'Under the greenwood tree' and 'Blow, blow, thou winter wind'. *As You Like It*

ANDROMACHE: Hector's wife. She despairingly tries to stop him going out to fight the Greeks. *Troilus and Cressida*

ANDRONICUS, MARCUS AND TITUS: *see* Marcus Andronicus and Titus Andronicus

ANGELO: A goldsmith who makes a chain for Antipholus of Ephesus, but gives it to his twin by mistake, then asks the former to pay for it. This sparks off some twinnish complications. *The Comedy of Errors*

Ordered by Duke Vincentio, who makes him his deputy, to enforce immorality laws during his pretended absence. Angelo condemns Claudio to death because he has seduced Juliet. He later tells Claudio's sister, Isabella, that if she will become his mistress her brother will be set free. Isabella, valuing her virginity to an appalling or saintly degree, depending on one's point of view, refuses, despite her brother's entreaties. However, the disguised Duke intervenes and persuades Isabella to pretend to give in to Angelo and visit his house, while the Duke arranges that Angelo's rejected fiancée, Mariana, shall be in Isabella's place in his bed. Angelo, though he is under the impression that he has enjoyed Isabella, still orders Claudio's death. The Duke steps in and forces Angelo to marry Mariana.
The rôle of Angelo has attracted major actors. He can be interpreted as a cold, stern Puritan brought down by lust, a tormented fanatic, a frightening villain, a hypocrite who outdoes Tartuffe, or a flawed ascetic, cruelty and sensuality being essentials to all readings. *Measure for Measure*

ANGUS: A Scottish noble who sides with Malcolm against Macbeth. *Macbeth*

ANNE, LADY: She encounters Richard as she laments over the dead Henry VI, her father-in-law, whom he has slain, as he had also earlier slain her husband, Edward, at

5

Tewkesbury. She curses him—'Blush, blush, thou lump of foul deformity'—but he begins to woo her, pretending he has killed her husband to win her. He offers his bared breast for her to stab. She becomes half-convinced, half-hypnotized by his words and agrees to marry him, but dies after her coronation in mysterious circumstances. Her ghost comes to haunt Richard before Bosworth.

The part, though not a large one is crucial because of the extraordinary wooing scene and the great emotional stress the actress must convey—and her gradual breakdown before Richard's fascination. *Richard III*

ANTENOR: A Trojan captured by the Greeks and exchanged for Cressida. A man of shrewd wit and soundest judgement, according to Pandarus. *Troilus and Cressida*

ANTIGONUS: A Sicilian lord, married to the splendidly outspoken Paulina. He, too, is prepared to speak his mind, telling Leontes firmly that he believes his queen Hermione is innocent of the charges against her. Forced by the King to abandon the alleged bastard infant Perdita in a remote place, he has the misfortune, after obeying orders, to be eaten. His demise is summed up in one of the most famous of all stage directions—'Exit, pursued by a bear'. *The Winter's Tale*

ANTIOCHUS: The King of Antioch who has proclaimed that anyone wishing to marry his daughter must first solve a riddle. Pericles discovers that the answer to the riddle is the King's incestuous relationship with his daughter. Fearing Pericles will reveal all, Antiochus tries to have him murdered, but is himself 'shrivell'd up' by a fire from heaven. *Pericles*

ANTIPHOLUS: They are identical twins, the sons of Aegeon and Aemilia. They have been separated in a shipwreck when they were infants and have grown up to be Antipholus of Ephesus and of Syracuse. Eighteen years after their separation, they both arrive in Ephesus on the same day, with their twin slaves, the Dromios. Aegeon also arrives, and a variety of complications ensue with the twins being mistaken for one another. They are finally reunited, but not before both have reached such a state of confusion that they are almost put away as lunatics. *The Comedy of Errors*

ANTONIO: A merchant of Venice. Asked by Bassanio to lend him 3,000 ducats so that he can pursue Portia, a rich heiress, Antonio borrows the money from Shylock, a rich Jewish moneylender he despises, using his ships and merchandise as a pledge. Shylock demands a pound of Antonio's flesh if he fails to pay up. News comes that Antonio's 'ships have all miscarried', and Shylock demands his pound of flesh. At the trial that follows, Portia, disguised as a lawyer, saves Antonio by telling Shylock that his life will be forfeit if a drop of Antonio's blood is shed. Shylock's fortune is decreed forfeit by the court, but Antonio requests that his enemy may keep half of it as long as he becomes a Christian and bequeaths his fortune to Lorenzo, his daughter, Jessica's, lover.

Antonio is not the easiest character for an actor to bring to life. His only friend seems to be Bassanio and he suffers from a strange melancholy. *The Merchant of Venice*.

The brother of Leonato. When the latter is grieving over his daughter, Hero's, shame and apparent death, Antonio tells him to 'make those that do offend you suffer too'. He proceeds to challenge Claudio, who has been tricked into jilting Hero, in the most violent language. But, finally, when he finds that 'all things sort so well', he gives his masked 'daughter' to a suitably repentant Claudio, who finds she is Hero. *Much Ado About Nothing*

Prospero's evil brother who usurps the Dukedom of Milan from him. He also puts Prospero and his daughter, Miranda, in 'a rotten carcass of a boat'. Later, he is ship-wrecked on the island where Prospero and Miranda have taken refuge. There, he attempts to kill Alonso, King of Naples, but is finally forced to restore Prospero's Dukedom to him. *The Tempest*

7

Sebastian's sea-captain friend, who comes to Illyria with him, despite the fact that the Duke Orsino is his enemy. He hands a purse to Sebastian and later mistakenly asks his twin, Viola, disguised as a boy, to return it after he has been arrested for fighting for her. He is taken before Orsino and only saved when all is explained. *Twelfth Night*

The father of Proteus. He sends him to the Emperor's court in Milan to make a perfect man of him. *Two Gentlemen of Verona*

ANTONY, MARK: Caesar's lieutenant and friend and, later, one of the triumvirs after his death. *Julius Caesar*

The play's hero. *Antony and Cleopatra*

He begins as a shrewd, high-living, buccaneering romantic. Before his master's death, he is drawn aside by one of the conspirators, Brutus having decided that he must be spared. His speeches on seeing Caesar's body are famous and moving, and Brutus unwisely gives him permission to speak at the funeral. Antony, left alone, promises to 'let slip the dogs of war'.
At the funeral, Antony, in one of the greatest speeches in drama, craftily and gradually turns the crowd into a frenzied mob. With Octavius Caesar and Lepidus he forms a triumvirate to defeat the killers and their sympathizers, but when Brutus and Cassius are both dead, it is Antony who movingly praises Brutus's pure motives and calls him the noblest Roman of them all. *Julius Caesar*

He has become 'the triple pillar of the world' transformed by Cleopatra into 'a strumpet's fool'. The part is now a great but very difficult one. Antony is talked of, and not only by Cleopatra, in terms of a god-like superman whose 'legs bestrid the ocean', whose voice when roused was like 'rattling thunder'. In his passion he is prepared to 'let Rome in Tiber melt'. He and Cleopatra, but especially Antony as the greatest living Roman, sacrifice everything for love. But we have to take Antony's greatness and

8

nobility on trust; we see little evidence of it, which is why few actors have triumphed in the rôle, which demands great acting and inspired casting.

We meet Antony at the beginning totally ensnared by Cleopatra and refusing to return to Rome. However, he goes back to face the threat of civil war and when he hears that his wife, Fulvia, has died. Soon he is quarrelling with Octavius Caesar, but the quarrel is settled by his marriage to Caesar's sister, Octavia. With Lepidus and Caesar he makes peace with Pompey, but later learns that Caesar has restarted the war and also imprisoned Lepidus. Octavia returns to Rome and Antony to Egypt. Caesar marches against him and Antony unwisely fights him at sea, fleeing after Cleopatra's ships have fled. He is ashamed, abuses her, but is soon reconciled.

He tries to parley with Caesar, then challenges him to personal combat. He has a messenger from Caesar whipped, abuses Cleopatra for receiving him, but is once more reconciled with her. Caesar refuses single combat and in the ensuing battle Antony is deserted by the Egyptians and is defeated. He rages against 'the foul Egyptian' who has betrayed him and she flees to her Monument and sends a message that she has killed herself. Antony begs his friend Eros to kill him but Eros kills himself instead and Antony, falling on his own sword, fails to die instantly. He is taken to Cleopatra and dies at her side. *Antony and Cleopatra*

APEMANTUS: A cynical and churlish philosopher who vainly warns the generous Timon that his friends are false. Timon discovers the worst and becomes even more of a misanthrope than Apemantus, who has a stone thrown at him after calling Timon 'too bad to curse'. *Timon of Athens*

APOTHECARY: He is poverty-stricken enough to break the law of Mantua by selling Romeo a dram of poison for forty ducats. *Romeo and Juliet*

ARCHIDAMUS: A Bohemian lord who opens the play with Camillo, discusses the King of Bohemia's visit to Sicilia, and does not appear again. *The Winter's Tale*

9

ARIEL: An 'airy', mischievous spirit, kept by a witch in a cloven pine until he is rescued by Prospero. He works for his liberator, organizing the storm that causes the shipwreck. He also lures Ferdinand to Miranda, while singing, 'Come unto these yellow sands', and wakes Gonzalo up in time to prevent the murder of King Alonso. He sings, 'Where the bee sucks, there suck I' while waiting to be released by Prospero from serving him, and when he has obeyed Prospero's instructions and found the supposedly wrecked ship and its lost crew, and also provided the necessary fair wind and calm sea for the voyage home, he is set free. This magical creature is by no means actor—or actress—proof. *The Tempest*

ARMADO, DON ADRIANO DE: A pompous, wordy, curiously fantastical Spanish noble, who is Costard's rival for the country wench, Jaquenetta, and who is mocked by the King and his friends. A letter he has written to Jaquenetta gets delivered to Rosaline and its flowery language is laughed at. The Don plays Hector in the 'Interlude of the Nine Worthies' and gets barracked by the courtiers. He ends the play after the singing is over with the magical lines, 'The words of Mercury are harsh after the songs of Apollo. You, that way: we this way.' *Love's Labour's Lost*

ARRAGON, PRINCE OF: One of Portia's suitors. He fails the test of the caskets, choosing the silver one which contains 'the portrait of a blinking idiot', and leaves feeling very foolish. *The Merchant of Venice*

ARTEMIDORUS OF CNIDOS: A teacher of rhetoric who, as Caesar passes on his way to the Capitol on the day of his death, gives him a note warning him of the conspiracy against him, and urges him to read it at once. Caesar asks if he is mad and passes on. *Julius Caesar*

ARTHUR: As in history, he has a better claim to the throne than his uncle, John, and is entrusted to Hubert de Burgh, who is ordered to kill him. Unable to bring himself to blind Arthur, as John's written orders insist, Hubert hides him and tells the King he is dead. Arthur later tries to escape by leaping from the walls of the castle where he is imprisoned, but falls to his death. *King John*

ARVIRAGUS AND GUIDERIUS: The sons of the King and the brothers of Imogen. The boys have been kidnapped as infants by Belarius to revenge himself on Cymbeline for banishing him. He brings them up, calling himself Morgan, Guiderius, Polydore and Arviragus, Cadwal. Imogen, dressed as a boy, later takes refuge with them, not knowing who they are, and when they find her apparently dead they speak the matchless verses over her body, beginning: 'Fear no more the heat o' the sun'. They help to repel the Romans and are reunited with their father. Guiderius, who is the elder, is perhaps even more rugged than his brother, judged by their speeches, and not simply because he kills Cloten, Imogen's step-brother, but both boys are equally brave. *Cymbeline*

ATHENIAN: An old man who wants Timon to stop his daughter marrying Timon's servant, Lucilius. Timon—not yet ruined and soured—finds that they love each other, and gets the old man's agreement to the match by providing Lucilius with suitable financial expectations. *Timon of Athens*

AUDREY: An ignorant and dim-witted country wench, who jilts her William for a more attractive prospect, Touchstone the Clown. He describes her as 'a poor virgin, an ill-favoured thing, but mine own'. He calls her a foul slut, to which she replies: 'I am not a slut, though I thank the gods that I am foul.' *As You Like It*

AUFIDIUS, TULLUS: The Volscian general and bitter enemy of Caius Marcius, later Coriolanus, until the latter is banished from Rome and seeks an alliance with him. The two march on Rome, but Coriolanus is swayed to spare the city by his family, and makes a treaty. When he returns with the spoils to the Volscians, the jealous Aufidius gathers a gang of conspirators and kills him. Aufidius is an eloquent hater, and a tough, proud, mailed fist of a man, but after the murder, his better self is revealed as he says: 'My rage is gone, And I am struck with sorrow.' *Coriolanus*

AUMERLE, DUKE OF; DUKE OF YORK:
Son of Edmund, Duke of York, and cousin of Richard II, whom he supports against Bolingbroke, also his cousin. Later, at Bolingbroke's—now Henry IV's—first Parliament, Aumerle is accused of murdering the Duke of Gloucester. Then, he is denounced by his father for treason against the new régime, but Henry pardons him. *Richard II*

Aumerle, now Duke of York, dies valiantly in the van of Agincourt, his death being vividly described by Exeter. *Henry V*

AUSTRIA, DUKE OF: *see* Lymoges

AUTOLYCUS: A pedlar, pickpocket and engagingly light-hearted rogue of Bohemia—an Elizabethan spiv *par excellence*. He is forced to change clothes with Florizel to help the latter's escape to Sicilia, then proceeds to extort money from the Shepherd and his Clown son. A singing rogue, his songs include: 'When daffodils begin to peer'. *The Winter's Tale*

AUVERGNE, COUNTESS OF: A Frenchwoman who tries to capture Lord Talbot, the English commander, in her castle. Having failed, and being impressed by him, she proceeds to feast him. *Henry VI*

B

BAGOT, SIR WILLIAM: With Bushy and Green he is described by Bolingbroke as one of 'the caterpillars of the commonwealth'. He accuses Aumerle of the murder of Gloucester. Unlike the other two, he survives. *Richard II*

BALTHASAR: A merchant invited to dinner with Antipholus of Ephesus. When his would-be host is locked out of his own house by his wife, Balthasar advises him not to get violent. *The Comedy of Errors*

A servant of Portia, who is sent to her cousin, Doctor Bellario, with a letter and sets off having uttered his only line. Portia later adopts his name when she pretends to be a lawyer. *The Merchant of Venice*

A servant of Don Pedro, who sings the song, 'Sigh no more, ladies' and is rather modest about his efforts. Benedick (aside) is very scathing. *Much Ado About Nothing*

Romeo's servant who, when his master is living in banishment in Mantua, brings him news of Juliet's apparent death. He later goes with him to the tomb of the Capulets, but, after meeting Friar Laurence, is caught outside by the Watch. *Romeo and Juliet*

BANQUO: A Scottish noble and general who helps Macbeth defeat the rebel, Macdonald, and his Norwegian allies. On their way home, they meet the Witches who tell Banquo that he will be the ancestor of Scottish kings. Because of this prophecy, Macbeth later orders his death, but his young son, Fleance, manages to escape. At a banquet, Banquo's ghost appears to haunt Macbeth. This noble-natured character is not historical. *Macbeth*

BAPTISTA MINOLA: A rich merchant of Padua and the father of Katharina, the Shrew, and of Bianca. He refuses to allow his favourite Bianca to be married until Katharina finds a husband, and is delighted when Petruchio appears and woos, weds and tames her. *The Taming of the Shrew*

BARDOLPH: He is one of Falstaff's cronies and his face is his misfortune, being covered with 'bubukles, and whelks, and knobs, and flames of fire'. When Falstaff looks at him he 'thinks upon hell-fire'. In the first play Bardolph helps in the robbery at Gadshill and marches north with Falstaff's 'ragged army'. In the second, as 'Corporate Bardolph', he assists in recruiting. *1 and 2 Henry IV*

Falstaff gets him made tapster of the Garter Inn. *The Merry Wives of Windsor*

He laments Falstaff's death and later gets hanged for looting French churches. *Henry V*

BARDOLPH, LORD: One of Northumberland's men, who brings him false news that his son, Hotspur, has won at Shrewsbury. Later, he appears to desert Northumberland, but his death, with his leader, is reported to the King. *2 Henry IV*

BARNARDINE: A 'dissolute prisoner', who has thoroughly enjoyed nine years in jail as a condemned murderer, continually reprieved, as he can be continually drunk there. The Duke tells the Provost to have him executed in place of Claudio, but Barnardine refuses, being drunk and unfit for such a state. Fortunately, another prisoner dies, whose head is used instead of Claudio's. Finally, the Duke pardons Barnardine, but hands him over to a Friar to deal with 'his stubborn soul'. *Measure for Measure*

BASSANIO: Antonio's cheerful friend, who borrows 3,000 ducats from him to court the wealthy Portia in appropriate style. Antonio gets the money from Shylock on the understanding that he will lose a pound of flesh if the money is not repaid. Bassanio goes to Belmont to woo Portia and passes the necessary test of choosing one of three caskets, selecting the lead one which has 'Who chooseth me must give and hazard all he hath' on it. Inside is Portia's picture and the two are betrothed.

Hearing that Antonio cannot pay Shylock, Portia sends Bassanio to him to offer him 6,000 ducats, but he refuses. Portia, disguised as a lawyer, turns the tables on Shylock and all ends happily for the newly-weds, after Bassanio has been teased by Portia about the ring he gave the 'lawyer' as a reward, which she had given him.

Despite recent interpretations of Bassanio as a caddish young man on the make, he would probably have seemed to Elizabethans as a sympathetic Renaissance aristocrat who runs up debts to the manner born. *The Merchant of Venice*

BASSET: A Lancastrian who quarrels with Vernon, a Yorkist. *1 Henry VI*

BASSIANUS: The younger brother of the Emperor Saturninus. He is in love with Titus's daughter, Lavinia, and when Saturninus says that he himself will make her his wife, seizes her, takes her away and marries her. He is later murdered by Demetrius and Chiron, sons of the vengeful Tamora, Queen of the Goths. He is a victim of a nightmarish plot against Titus and all his family. *Titus Andronicus*

BATES, JOHN: An English soldier at Agincourt, who appears in the scene between the disguised Henry and some of his men on the night before the battle. Though he wishes that the King were there alone 'so should sure to be ransomed, and many a poor men's lives saved', he determines 'to fight lustily for him', and tells the King and Williams not to quarrel, as 'we have French quarrels enow'. *Henry V*

BAWD: The keeper of a brothel in Mytilene and wife of the Pandar. Boult, their servant, brings her the innocent Marina, whose invincible virginity brings the wretched Madam to near-despair. Finally, she tells Boult to 'crack the glass' of the said virginity and 'make the rest malleable'. But even Boult is overcome by Marina's goodness—and a bribe—into helping her out of the clutches of the 'cursed Bawd'. *Pericles*

BEATRICE AND BENEDICK: She is Antonio's niece and Hero's cousin and he is a lord of Padua and a soldier. She and her verbal sparring partner in their 'merry war' are officially 'sub plot', yet they have always been *Much Ado*'s hero and heroine. Lines of Thomas Digges, who died in 1635, confirm this. If they are on the bill, 'The Cockpit, Galleries, Boxes, are all full.'

Beatrice, who says of herself, 'There was a star danced, and under that was I born', claims to be a confirmed spinster, while Benedick claims to be a confirmed bachelor. Greatly attracted to each other, they hide their feelings under 'a skirmish of wit'. Benedick calls Beatrice 'My Lady Disdain'. Their friends decide to take a hand. Benedick overhears an apparently accidental conversation between Don Pedro, Leonato and Claudio, who say that Beatrice is dying of love for him but will 'die ere she make herself known'. Beatrice is tricked in the same way by Hero and Ursula. They admit their love, but Beatrice tests Benedick by demanding that he kill Claudio for slandering Hero. Benedick is reluctant but finally agrees. Fortunately, Claudio finds he has wronged Hero, there is no need for the duel, and Beatrice and Benedick arrange to be married at the same time as Hero and Claudio.

Dover Wilson called Beatrice the first woman in English literature to have a brain and delight in its constant employment. In this, Benedick is almost, but not quite, her match. *Much Ado About Nothing*

BEAUFORT, HENRY: The great-uncle of Henry VI, the Bishop of Winchester and, later, a Cardinal. He is the rival of the Protector, Gloucester, who claims he has murdered Henry V. He crowns Henry VI in Paris. *1 Henry VI*

He helps bring about the disgrace of Gloucester's wife, the Duke's arrest for alleged treason and his death. Beaufort's short death scene, with Warwick arguing that 'So bad a death argues a monstrous life', is worthy of the later Shakespeare. *2 Henry VI*

BEAUFORT, THOMAS: The younger brother of the Cardinal. He appears as the Duke of Exeter, uncle of the King, who urges him to claim the French crown. He arrests the traitors Cambridge, Scroop and Grey and is sent as ambassador to the French King to demand his submission. He is at Harfleur and Agincourt. *Henry V*

He is the new King's guardian who seeks peace and foresees the horrors of the Wars of the Roses, hoping he may die before that 'hapless time' begins. *1 Henry VI*

BEAUFORT, JOHN: The Earl, and, later, the 1st Duke of Somerset, and a nephew of the above two Beauforts. In the Temple Garden, he quarrels with Richard Plantagenet, Duke of York, who picks a white rose and invites his supporters to do the same. Whereupon, Somerset picks a red one. *1 Henry VI*

BEAUFORT, EDMUND: This younger brother of John and 2nd Duke of Somerset carries on the quarrel with York. During his spell as Regent of France most English possessions are lost, and York demands his removal and has him put in the Tower. Furious when he finds Somerset with Queen Margaret, York fights the Lancastrians, thus starting the Wars of the Roses, and kills Somerset at St. Albans. *2 and 3 Henry VI*

The younger brother of Henry Beaufort, 3rd Duke of Somerset, whom he succeeds as 4th Duke. He joins Warwick's army after Edward IV's marriage to Lady Grey and is captured and executed at Tewkesbury. 'Off with his guilty head!' shouts the King. *3 Henry VI*

BEDFORD, JOHN, DUKE OF LANCASTER: The third son of Henry IV. He appears briefly and gallantly at the Battle of Shrewsbury and is sent to fight the Northern rebels. *1 Henry IV*. He is not so gallant, capturing them by a trick and, having got them to dismiss their troops and promising to right their wrongs, treacherously arrests them and has them executed. *2 Henry IV*. Now Duke of Bedford, he appears (unhistorically) at Agincourt. *Henry V*. He is Regent of France. He captures Orleans and Rouen, where he dies and is buried. *1 Henry VI*

BELARIUS: He is a good old man, unjustly banished, living in the wilds of Wales under the name of Morgan. Twenty years earlier he has revenged himself on Cymbeline by kidnapping his two sons, Guiderius and Arviragus, and reared them as his own sons. He is worried because the boys show signs of their princely natures, despite their rough upbringing. He joins them in fighting the Romans and helps to swing the battle to Cymbeline's cause. Then, he reveals his secret to the King when Guiderius is threatened with execution, and is completely restored to favour. *Cymbeline*

BELCH, SIR TOBY: The jovial, tippling, coarse, old uncle of Olivia, and a hanger-on in her household. He gulls Sir Andrew into thinking Olivia may love him and guides him through drunken revels. Together with Maria, Olivia's gentlewoman, they conspire to make her pompous steward, Malvolio, believe that his mistress adores him. Sir Toby then encourages the cowardly Sir Andrew to challenge Viola, disguised as a man and his supposed rival for Olivia. By the end of the play the old reprobate is £2,000 better off —thanks to Sir Andrew—and has married Maria as a reward for her part in the downfall of Malvolio. *Twelfth Night*

BENEDICK: *see* Beatrice and Benedick

BENVOLIO: Romeo's cousin and friend. A likable young man who fights when he has to, but tries to keep the peace. His common sense is reflected when he tells Mercutio that they should leave the Verona square—'The day is hot, the Capulets abroad.' He urges Romeo to flee after killing Tybalt and tells the Prince how it happened, then disappears from the play. *Romeo and Juliet*

BERKELEY, EARL: He is reprimanded by Bolingbroke for calling him 'My Lord of Hereford' instead of Lancaster, the title he claims. Berkeley has come from the Duke of York to ask the reason for Bolingbroke's arrival to 'fright our native peace with self-borne arms'. *Richard II*

BERNARDO: An officer who, with Marcellus, has twice seen the ghost of Hamlet's father, then brings Horatio to see it. They tell Hamlet about the apparition, then Bernardo disappears from the play. *Hamlet*

BEROWNE OR BIRON: One of three young noblemen who, with their King, agree to study, and to avoid women, for three years. He is the wittiest and most sceptical of the quartet. However, one by one, they succumb to the Princess of France and her companions, and Berowne, who has fallen in love with Rosaline, justifies their weakness in a magnificent speech, and tells them that their original vow was 'Flat treason 'gainst the kingly state of youth.' He finally urges them to 'Advance your standards, and upon them, lords! Pell-mell, down with them.'

His Rosaline's wit is sometimes even sharper than his own, and the two have been cited as foreshadowing the 'merry war' of Beatrice and Benedick. But Berowne, one of the finest rôles in early Shakespeare, is no shadow of anyone. He is an early example of the Shakespeare Man, those characters into which the playwright, for all his neutrality, seems to have poured so much of himself. *Love's Labour's Lost*

BERTRAM: The son of the Countess of Rousillon, who is forced by the King of France into marrying Helena, who adores him. She has cured the grateful King of illness. Bertram not only does not love her, but thinks she is not good enough for him, and refuses to bed her. He goes off campaigning with the bitter line, which some suggest is Shakespeare speaking of his own marriage: 'War is no strife To the dark house and the detested wife.' He tells her he will only accept her if she can get a ring off his finger and also 'show me a child begotten of thy body that I am father to'. In Florence he tries to seduce a girl named Diana, into whose bed Helena manages to creep and get both ring and child. So finally Bertram accepts her.

Even though Bertram has Helena forced on him very much against his will, he is so boorish and such an anti-hero that he is considered to have stood in the way of the play's popularity. *All's Well that Ends Well*

BIANCA: The mistress of Cassio. Though her actual rôle is small, it is a key one, for she unwittingly helps bring about Othello's downfall. Cassio gives Desdemona's handker-chief, which has been planted in his lodgings by Iago to

Bianca, and Othello sees her returning it to him. Iago later manages to make Othello think that he and Cassio are talking about Desdemona when in fact they are discussing Bianca. *Othello*

The younger and better tempered daughter of Baptista Minola, her elder sister being Katharina, the Shrew. Bianca is not allowed suitors until Katharina is wed. However, she elopes with Lucentio after he has seen her disguised as a schoolmaster. In the final scene she proves less obedient to him than the erstwhile Shrew is to Petruchio. *The Taming of the Shrew*

BIGOT, LORD: One of those who find Arthur's body and assume that Hubert, acting on the King's orders, is responsible. 'Out dunghill!' he roars at Hubert, when he sees him. With Pembroke and Salisbury he joins the Dauphin, but returns to John's banner when the three find they are to be executed by the Dauphin after he has used them to defeat the English. *King John*

BIONDELLO: A servant of Lucentio. When his master changes identity with Tranio so that he can get to see Bianca, Biondello acts as Tranio's servant to support the plot. A small part which runs through the play. *The Taming of the Shrew*

BLANCH: The daughter of the King of Castile and the niece of John. She marries the Dauphin, which leads to an alliance between France and England, but when John is excommunicated the alliance is shattered. Blanch, in several short, moving speeches, voices her despair—'The sun's o'ercast with blood'—but sides with her husband: 'There where my fortune lives, there my life dies.' *King John*

BLUNT, SIR WALTER: A loyal supporter of the King, who sends him to Hotspur before the Battle of Shrewsbury to bid him and his fellow rebels 'name their griefs'. In the fight, dressed as the King, he is killed by Douglas. *1 Henry IV*

BLUNT, SIR JOHN: The son of Sir Walter. A wordless rôle, he is ordered by John of Lancaster to guard Sir John Colville. *2 Henry IV*

BLUNT, SIR JAMES: The grandson of Sir Walter, and a captain in Richmond's army. *Richard III*

BOATSWAIN: A fine sailor, beset by interfering nobles in the storm that opens the play. He tells them just what he thinks of them, saying they 'do assist the storm'. *The Tempest*

BOLINGBROKE, HENRY: *see* Henry IV

BOLINGBROKE: A 'conjuror', who, with several accomplices, calls up a spirit for the Duchess of Gloucester, who hopes her husband will be king. The rites are interrupted by York and Buckingham, and Bolingbroke is condemned to death. *2 Henry VI*

BONA: The sister of the French Queen. Warwick has arranged for her to marry Edward IV. When news is brought that Edward has married Lady Grey, Bona urges the King of France to aid Margaret, the deposed Henry VI's wife, in her struggle against Edward. *3 Henry VI*

BORACHIO: A follower of the evil Don John. It is he who suggests to his master the plot that will bring about the downfall of Hero, who is to marry Claudio. He woos Margaret, deceiving the watching Claudio into thinking she is Hero. He is later arrested by Dogberry and the Watch and finally confesses to Don Pedro, demanding 'nothing but the reward of a villain', but he clears Margaret of all blame. *Much Ado About Nothing*

BOTTOM, NICK: An Athenian weaver and the star of a small company of 'mechanicals' who rehearse, and later play, 'Pyramus and Thisbe' before the Duke. A simple soul, rather engagingly conceited, nothing shakes his superb complacency. He is upset when Peter Quince, the director, will not let him play the lion as well as Pyramus: clearly he would like to play all the parts.

When Puck gives him an ass's head and Titania, under a spell, falls in love with him, Bottom accepts the situation and makes small talk with the fairies. Translated back again to his own shape in time for the performance, he is not the least put out by rude comments from his aristocratic audience: his self-satisfaction is invincible. *A Midsummer Night's Dream*

BOULT: The servant of the Pandar and the Bawd who run the brothel in Mytilene. He brings the virgin Marina there, but when she seems about to ruin the establishment by converting its clients to chastity, he cries: 'Faith, I must ravish her, or she'll disfurnish us of all our cavaliers.' Marina escapes by bribing Boult to place her in a respectable house amongst honest women, though he admits his 'acquaintance lies little amongst them'. *Pericles*

BOURBON, JOHN, DUKE OF: He is captured at Agincourt, having earlier urged attacking the English, whom he calls 'Normans, but bastard Normans'. *Henry V*

BOURCHIER, CARDINAL: He is browbeaten by Buckingham into agreeing to remove the young Duke of York and the Queen Mother from sanctuary. He is the Archbishop of Canterbury. *Richard III*

BOY: As Page to Falstaff, he is put into the fat knight's service by Prince Hal. He appears in a number of scenes and speaks up for himself boldly. *2 Henry IV*

He summons Pistol and the Hostess to help get his sick master to bed and asks Bardolph of the flaming face to put his head between the sheets to act as a warming pan. Later, he goes to Harfleur as Boy to Pistol, Bardolph and Nym, but decides to leave them, as he is tired of their constant thieving. Nym and Bardolph are both hanged and the boy reappears at Agincourt with Pistol and interprets for him when he is captured by a Frenchman. He then decides to help guard the luggage of the camp with the other boys and is presumably killed there when the French attack it. *Henry V*

He is probably ROBIN, who carries Falstaff's love letters to the wives. Sent by his master to attend Mrs. Page, he says he would rather go before her 'like a man than follow like a dwarf' and from then on joins in the plot against him. *The Merry Wives of Windsor*

BOY, SON TO MACDUFF: His mother tells him of his father's death, then he is murdered in front of her after bravely standing up to one of the murderers. *Macbeth*

BOYET: A lord attending the Princess of France. This smooth-talking dandy does little but act as a messenger, though he lets the Princess and her ladies know that the masked visitors from Muscovy are, in fact, the King and his friends. *Love's Labour's Lost*

BRABANTIO: The father of Desdemona, who, in the Senate scene, accuses Othello of stealing his daughter. He finally and reluctantly accepts the match, but warns the Moor that she may deceive him as she has deceived her father. Later, we learn that he has died of grief. *Othello*

BRAKENBURY, SIR ROBERT: The Lieutenant of the Tower who reluctantly surrenders the sleeping Duke of Clarence to the two murderers sent by Richard to kill him. Later, he presumably gives up the two young Princes to Tyrel. He is reported killed at Bosworth. *Richard III*

BRANDON: *see* Suffolk, Duke of

BRANDON, SIR WILLIAM: He is ordered by Richmond to bear his standard at Bosworth, where he is killed. *Richard III*

BRUTUS, DECIUS: A conspirator against Caesar. At the conspirators' meeting he says he can 'o'ersway' Caesar if the omens are unfavourable for his visit to the Capitol. When Caesar the following morning tells him he will stay away because of a bad omen, Decius re-interprets the all-too-accurate dream of Caesar's wife, Calpurnia, tells him the Senate are waiting to crown him, and makes him change his mind. His final master-stroke is to suggest that Caesar will be mocked if he stays away from fear. After the murder, Decius disappears from the play. *Julius Caesar*

BRUTUS, JUNIUS: He and SICINIUS VELUTUS are tribunes of the people, 'the tongues o' the common mouth', as Coriolanus calls them. They stir the populace against him and bring about his banishment, though these effective rabble-rousers resist the call for his death. When Coriolanus leads the Volscians against Rome, however, the pair have the gall to deny having wronged him and try to persuade Menenius to stop Coriolanus from attacking the city. *Coriolanus*

BRUTUS, MARCUS: The idealistic leader of the conspiracy against Caesar. He is a noble and tragic figure who many regard as the hero of the play. He joins the conspirators not out of envy, like Cassius, or malice, but because he sees it his duty to rid Rome of a man he loves, but who may become a tyrant if he is crowned.

Throughout his first scene, Cassius works on Brutus's concern about the enormous power of Caesar and his ambition. When we next meet him, he has decided that Caesar must die, but he tells the conspirators that they do not have to swear on oath—their cause does not need it—and that Antony must be spared: they are sacrificers, not butchers. When Portia, his wife, asks him to confide in her, he will not. He is the last to stab Caesar—'*Et tu*, Brute? Then fall, Caesar!*' He unwisely allows Antony to speak at the funeral, and, after his own sensible, explanatory speech, Antony turns the crowd into a mob.

Civil War breaks out and we next find him quarrelling at Sardis with Cassius whom he accuses of taking bribes. They are reconciled and Brutus tells Cassius that Portia has committed suicide. Against Cassius's wishes, Brutus chooses to fight at Philippi. After a stormy confrontation with Octavius and Antony, Brutus and Cassius say an 'everlasting farewell' and are defeated. Brutus asks his servant to kill him. Finally, Strato agrees and 'the noblest

Roman of them all' as Antony later calls him, runs onto his own sword. *Julius Caesar*

BUCKINGHAM, HUMPHREY STAFFORD, 1st DUKE OF: He is mainly responsible for finding out that the Duchess of Gloucester practices sorcery and helps to get the Duke of Gloucester disgraced. He later falsely promises that the followers of Jack Cade will be pardoned. A supporter of Henry VI against the Yorkists when the Wars of the Roses breaks out. *2 Henry VI*. He is reported killed in the first battle. *3 Henry VI*

BUCKINGHAM, HENRY STAFFORD, 2nd DUKE OF: He is grandson of the above and Gloucester's chief supporter, secretly, at first, while he pretends to be friendly with Edward IV and his family, but later publicly. He and Richard whom he wrongly believes he can dominate, have Rivers, Grey, Vaughan and Lord Hastings killed, and it is Buckingham who publicly engineers the accession of Gloucester as Richard III. However, the idea of killing the two little princes is too much for him, and his hesitation infuriates Richard. Buckingham attempts to join Richmond but, as Catesby exultantly tells the King, is captured. He has a final scene before he is led to 'the block of shame', then a ghostly appearance to Richard on the night before Bosworth. *Richard III*

BUCKINGHAM, EDWARD STAFFORD, 3rd DUKE OF: The son of the above who also ends his life on the block. With his son-in-law, Lord Abergavenny, he is arrested for high treason on the evidence of his surveyor who accuses him of threatening to kill the King, the arrest being arranged by his enemy, Wolsey, whom he characterizes as a venom-mouth'd butcher's cur. On his way to his death he proclaims his innocence to the crowd. *Henry VIII*

BULLCALF, PETER: He claims to be 'a diseased man' with 'a whoreson cold, sir; a cough, sir', to try and prevent himself being pressed into the King's service by Falstaff and Shallow. It does him no good, but he later escapes by

25

buying his release with a handsome bribe to Bardolph. *2 Henry IV*

BULLEN, ANNE: Henry's second wife. He meets her at a Masque at the home of Cardinal Wolsey and soon makes her the Marchioness of Pembroke. She is a shadowy figure in the play, though sympathetically drawn, for after Act II, in which she tells a sceptical old lady that she would not be queen for all the world, she has no lines, merely being seen in her own coronation procession, but not at the christening of her daughter, Elizabeth. *Henry VIII*

BURGUNDY, DUKE OF: He acts as a peacemaker between Henry and Charles VI of France, appearing in only one scene where he has a magnificent speech on the effect of war on 'fertile France'. *Henry V*

He is allied with the English and calls Joan of Arc a 'vile fiend and shameless courtezan!' But Joan appeals to him personally and, to the joy of the French King and his nobles, he changes sides. *1 Henry VI*

He has a tiny, not very attractive part in the first scene, being a suitor of Cordelia until she is cursed by her father and disinherited, at which point he excuses himself and leaves for home. *King Lear*

BUSHY: One of the King's three favourites, 'the caterpillars of the commonwealth', as Bolingbroke calls them, the other two being Bagot and Green. He and Green are executed at Bolingbroke's orders after being caught at Bristol. *Richard II*

BUTTS, DOCTOR: The King's Physician who shows Henry how badly Cranmer is being treated. *Henry VIII*

C

CADE, JACK: A rebel who, egged on by York, claims to be John Mortimer, heir to the throne. A splendidly uproarious rabble-rouser, he storms his way to London, promising, amongst other things, to abolish money and ordering his men to 'burn all the records of the realm: my mouth shall be the Parliament of England'. Clifford and Buckingham manage to make the rebel's followers desert him by appeals to their patriotism, and Cade flees to Kent where he is killed by Alexander Iden. *2 Henry VI*

CAESAR, JULIUS: The name part, if not the hero, of the play: if there is a hero, it is Brutus. Caesar, the master of the Roman world, is presented puzzlingly. Some find him weak and boastful, others noble. His spirit certainly can be said to dominate the play after his death—'O Julius Caesar! Thou art mighty yet,' says Brutus.

At the beginning he is back in Rome after defeating Pompey, and a Soothsayer tells him to beware the Ides of March. A conspiracy to kill him is led by his friend, Brutus, who fears his ambition and that he may become a tyrant if he is crowned. The night before his death, his wife, Calphurnia's, nightmares almost persuade him to stay at home, though he finely attacks cowardice: 'Cowards die many times before their deaths. The valiant never taste of death but once.' Decius Brutus, a conspirator, re-interprets Calphurnia's dream, and he decides to go to the Capitol, warned once more as he goes by the Soothsayer. In the Senate he is murdered, the last blow being struck by Brutus. Later, before Philippi, his Ghost haunts Brutus. *Julius Caesar*

CAESAR, OCTAVIUS: He becomes a triumvir with Antony and Lepidus after his great-uncle is assassinated. He and Antony defeat Brutus and Cassius at Philippi. *Julius Caesar*

He is portrayed as ambitious, cold, able and ruthless. We meet him criticizing Antony, 'our great competitor', to Lepidus. When Antony returns to Rome the two finally resolve their differences when Agrippa suggests that Antony should marry Octavius's sister, Octavia. They make peace with Pompey, but when Antony returns to

Egypt and Cleopatra, Octavius first imprisons Lepidus and renews the war against Pompey, then sets out to destroy Antony. He defeats him at sea at Actium, refuses a challenge to meet him in single combat, then defeats him again at Alexandria. With the lovers committing suicide, Octavius is left supreme. He officially laments 'a pair so famous': he can afford to. *Antony and Cleopatra*

CAITHNESS: A Scottish noble in Malcolm's army. *Macbeth*

CAIUS: A (silent) relative of Titus who shoots an arrow, on his instructions, with a message to Saturn attached to it. *Titus Andronicus*

CAIUS, DOCTOR: An irate French doctor in love with Anne Page. He challenges Sir Hugh Evans when he learns that the Welsh parson prefers Slender as a suitor for Anne. The Host of the Garter Inn sends them to different spots, which makes them unite against him and relieve him of three horses. Mrs. Page approves of Caius and arranges for Anne to be carried off by him during the teasing of Falstaff in Windsor Park, but Anne and Fenton arrange things so that the unfortunate doctor finds he has married a boy. 'By gar, I am cozened,' he roars. 'By gar, I shall raise all Windsor.' *The Merry Wives of Windsor*

CAIUS LUCIUS: He commands the Roman invaders of Britain. He comes there first as the Emperor Augustus Caesar's ambassador to demand the 'yearly three thousand pounds' of tribute money. When Cymbeline refuses, Lucius, an honourable and straightforward man, is forced to declare war. Later, he finds Imogen, Cymbeline's daughter, disguised as the boy, Fidele, and takes her into his service. When he is defeated by the Britons and captured he pleads for Fidele, 'a Britain born', and Cymbeline agrees to spare the 'youth'. But Imogen disowns Lucius as a Roman and he is only spared by Cymbeline after the King has recognized and been reunited with his daughter. *Cymbeline*

CAIUS MARCIUS: see Coriolanus

CALCHAS: A Trojan priest and the father of Cressida. He has gone over to the Greeks, and, when the Trojan general Antenor is captured, Calchas asks for Cressida, still in Troy, to be exchanged for him. When she joins Calchas, he does not hesitate to hand her over to Diomedes to be seduced. *Troilus and Cressida*

CALIBAN: The deformed, brutish offspring of a witch and an evil spirit. When Prospero is shipwrecked on the island, he finds this 'thing of darkness', teaches him to speak and makes him his slave. Caliban plans to murder his master with the help of Stephano and Trinculo, but they fail and Caliban decides to be 'wise hereafter and seek for grace'. Brutish as he is, he at least knows no better, unlike some of the unsavoury characters in the play, and Shakespeare gives him a most beautiful and haunting speech, beginning: 'Be not afeard: the isle is full of noises, Sounds and sweet airs, that give delight, and hurt not.' *The Tempest*

CALPHURNIA: Caesar's childless wife. She urges him not to 'stir out of your house today' after suffering terrifying dreams and hearing of alarming omens. Caesar finally agrees, but Decius Brutus, one of the conspirators, arrives and re-interprets her nightmare of Caesar's statue spouting blood and he goes to his death. *Julius Caesar*

CAMBRIDGE, RICHARD, EARL OF: He, Scroop and Grey conspire to murder the King when he is at Southampton *en route* for France. However, their plan has leaked out and Henry confronts them with their treason and, despite their pleas for mercy, has them executed. *Henry V*

CAMILLO: An old lord of Sicilia. Leontes, King of Sicilia, makes him swear to poison Polixenes, whom he suspects quite wrongly of being the lover of his wife, Hermione. Camillo warns Polixenes that, 'I am appointed to murder you' and they leave together for Bohemia. Sixteen years later, Polixenes, helped by a now homesick Camillo, finds that his son, Florizel, loves the shepherd girl, Perdita (actually the daughter of Leontes). When Polixenes refuses to allow the match, Camillo helps the pair to fly to Sicilia. At the end, the 'worth and honesty' of the good old man are noted by Leontes and everyone else. *The Winter's Tale*

CAMPEIUS, CARDINAL: The Italian Papal Legate, ordered by the Pope to investigate the problem of Katharine of Aragon's divorce. He is annoyed with Wolsey for engineering the dismissal of Henry's secretary, Dr. Pace. In an aside at the Queen's trial Henry complains that Campeius, who has asked for a postponement, is trifling with him, and mutters about the 'dilatory sloth and tricks of Rome'. Later, Campeius advises Katharine to give in to the 'loving and gracious' King's demands. *Henry VIII*

CANIDIUS: The Lieutenant-General of Antony's army. Before the Battle of Actium he urges his master to fight on land, not at sea. Bitterly, he tells a soldier 'we are women's men', meaning Cleopatra, who wants a sea-fight. His worst fears are realized, and stunned by Antony's flight, he decides 'to Caesar will I render My legions and my horse'. *Antony and Cleopatra*

CANTERBURY, ARCHBISHOP OF: He lets the audience know that the Prince Hal of the 'Henry IV' play is a reformed man. So as to forestall having half the Church's property confiscated under a law passed in the previous reign, the Archbishop encourages Henry to claim the French Throne, telling him that the Church will raise 'such a mighty sum As never did the clergy bring in to any of your ancestors'. Even Shakespeare occasionally nodded, like Homer, and the Archbishop's speech justifying Henry's claim is considered by F. E. Halliday 'perhaps the most tedious speech in Shakespeare'. *Henry V*

CAPHIS: A Senator's servant who is sent to Timon to ask him for the 'moneys' that he owes. Timon cannot pay. *Timon of Athens*

CAPTAIN: He takes written instructions from Edmund to hang Cordelia, but Lear later says he has killed him. *King Lear*

CAPTAIN OF A BAND OF WELSHMEN: He disperses his men, believing Richard dead. *Richard II*

CAPUCIUS: Charles V's Ambassador to England. He visits the dying Katharine of Aragon and brings her sympathetic messages from the King. She asks him to take Henry a letter commending their daughter, Mary, and her 'wretched women'. *Henry VIII*

CAPULET: Juliet's father and head of the family at enmity with the Montagues. An explosive but by no means unlikable man, very much master of his own household, his determination to marry Juliet to Paris brings about the tragedy. But, for all his hot temper, we believe him when he finds her apparently dead and says: 'And with my child my joys are buried.' When she and Romeo are finally dead he ends the feud with the Montagues. His speech of welcome to the Capulets' Ball beginning: 'Welcome, gentlemen! ladies that have their toes Unplagu'd by corns will walk a bout with you' is a joy. *Romeo and Juliet*

CAPULET, LADY: Juliet's mother, as anxious as her husband to see her married to Paris. She tries to restrain Capulet from setting upon the Montagues himself in the first scene, telling him he should have a crutch, not a sword. She does her best to praise Paris's virtues to Juliet, and, after Tybalt is slain it is she rather than her husband who urges the Prince to punish Romeo. She is utterly overcome by Juliet's apparent death and stricken with resigned despair at her actual death. *Romeo and Juliet*

CARLISLE, BISHOP OF: A loyal supporter of the King. He tries to cheer Richard after his return from Ireland to a rebellious England and surrenders with him to Bolingbroke, and he publicly protests when the usurper says he will take the throne. He takes part in a plot to kill Bolingbroke, but is pardoned by the latter because he has 'High sparks of honour' in him. *Richard II*

CASCA: One of the conspirators. Characterized by Brutus as blunt and Cassius for his 'sour manner', he gives an

31

amusing account to the two of how Caesar has refused the crown; but all his humour has departed when he meets Cicero in the next scene and describes a tempest he has seen 'dropping fire'. Cassius pulls him to his senses and it is Casca who is the first to stab Caesar, after which he does not appear again. *Julius Caesar*

CASSANDRA: The prophetess daughter of King Priam of Troy, and Hector's sister. On her first appearance she enters 'raving' to foretell the fall of Troy. Later, she tries to stop Hector fighting Achilles. *Troilus and Cressida*

CASSIO: He incurs the envy of Iago, Othello's ensign, when he is appointed the Moor's lieutenant. A likable man, he is no match for the malevolent Iago. He has 'very poor unhappy brains for drinking', and is made fighting drunk by Iago and so disgraced and dismissed by Othello, to whom he is utterly loyal. Iago suggests that Cassio should ask Desdemona, Othello's wife, to intercede with him, meanwhile poisoning the Moor's mind with the lie that Cassio and Desdemona are lovers. Iago then contrives that a handkerchief given to Desdemona by Othello shall be found on Cassio. Having convinced the Moor of Cassio's guilt he arranges to have him murdered by Roderigo, who fails. Cassio's innocence is not finally established until Othello kills Desdemona. Before Othello kills himself, Cassio is made governor of Cyprus in his place by Lodovico. Loyal to the end, Cassio's final words are 'for he was great of heart'. *Othello*

CASSIUS: This soldier-statesman originates the plot against Caesar, partly from sheer jealousy—unlike his friend Brutus—and partly because 'this man has now become a god'. He is characterized by Caesar as having a 'lean and hungry look' and one who, because he thinks too much, is dangerous. He is flawed by envy, anger and hatred, but is also very human, deeply attached to Brutus and easily hurt. To make more sure of Brutus's co-operation in the conspiracy, he decides to write letters 'in several hands', all allegedly from citizens who fear Caesar's ambition, and throw them through Brutus's window. It is Cassius who calms Casca, scared by omens, and who has the good sense to say that Antony must be killed, which Brutus forbids. Again, after the murder, it is Cassius who does not want Antony to be allowed to address the crowd, and again he is proved right.

He and Brutus are forced to flee. We next meet them in camp near Sardis where they quarrel over a man convicted of bribery and Brutus accuses his friend of having 'an itching palm'. Cassius is reduced to offering his bared breast to be stabbed, but the quarrel ends with the news that Brutus's wife has killed herself, and Cassius admires his self-control. He allows Brutus to get his way over fighting Octavius and Antony at Philippi, and, when the battle is lost, he has his newly-freed slave, Pindarus, kill him. *Julius Caesar*

CATESBY, SIR WILLIAM: A leading henchman of Richard. He is sent to test the feelings of Hastings and finds him loyal to the boy, Edward V. He helps in the charade by which the Lord Mayor and citizens of London are gulled into thinking Richard full of holy fervour, and later brings Richard the news that Buckingham, who has turned against the King, has been captured, but that Richmond is 'on the seas'. At Bosworth, he begs Richard to 'Withdraw, my lord: I'll help you to a horse.' *Richard III*

CATO, YOUNG: The son of Marcus Cato. He dies fighting bravely at Philippi for Brutus and Cassius. *Julius Caesar*

CELIA: The daughter of Duke Frederick who has usurped his brother's dominions and forced him into exile in the Forest of Arden. She is the devoted friend of her cousin, Rosalind, daughter of the banished Duke, and the play's heroine. When Frederick banishes Rosalind, Celia goes with her and she suggests to Rosalind that they look for her father. Rosalind goes dressed as a boy, Celia as a girl called Aliena. In the forest, where Rosalind finds her beloved Orlando, Celia meets her fate in the shape of Orlando's brother, Oliver, once hostile, but now friendly to him. The wooing of Celia and Oliver is off-stage and, as far as lines go, she fades from the play towards the end. *As You Like It*

CERES: A spirit summoned by Prospero to represent the various fruits of the harvest in a masque performed at the betrothal ceremonies for Ferdinand and Miranda. Told by Iris to bring wealth and prosperity to them, she and Juno sing to them. *The Tempest*

CERIMON: A rich lord of Ephesus, who is also a famous and much admired physician. To him is brought the apparently dead Thaisa, wife of Pericles, who thought her dead in childbirth at sea. Cerimon revives her and helps her to become a priestess of Diana. When, years later, Pericles reaches Ephesus, Cerimon confirms Thaisa's identity to him. *Pericles*

CESARIO: The name Viola adopts when she disguises herself as a page to serve Orsino. *Twelfth Night*

CHAMBERLAIN: The chamberlain of a Rochester Inn, who is in league with Falstaff's gang. He tells Gadshill when a rich franklin and his men will be setting out and is promised 'a share in our purchase'. *1 Henry IV*

CHARLES: Duke Frederick's wrestler. Oliver, Orlando's brother, hears the Court news from him, then does his best to inflame him against Orlando, hoping Charles will break his neck in a wrestling bout. In the event, Charles himself is thrown and carried out speechless. *As You Like It*

CHARLES VI: The King of France who makes a treaty with Henry after Agincourt in which he grants the English King the hand of his daughter, Katharine. Henry thus becomes heir to the French throne. *Henry V*

CHARLES VII: First the Dauphin, then the King of France. He fights with Joan La Pucelle (Joan of Arc) to test her out, is defeated and at once falls in love with her. When she is captured by the English he swears fealty to Henry. *1 Henry VI*

CHARMIAN: One of Cleopatra's attendants, who appears in a number of scenes. She is told by the soothsayer that she will outlive Cleopatra, but it proves to be for only a few moments: she kills herself in the same way as her mistress—with an asp—but not before uttering a supreme epitaph: 'Now boast thee, death, in thy possession lies A lass unparallel'd.' *Antony and Cleopatra*

CHATILLON: The French ambassador who threatens John with war if he does not abdicate in favour of his nephew, Arthur. He appears once more to tell Philip of France that John has invaded France. *King John*

CHIRON AND DEMETRIUS: Younger sons of Tamora, the vengeful Queen of the Goths, who rape Lavinia, cut off her hands and cut out her tongue. They manage to have Titus's sons, Quintus and Martius, executed for the murder of Bassianus, who they themselves have killed. These monsters meet a monstrous fate. Their throats are cut by Titus, and he has them baked in a pie and served to their mother. *Titus Andronicus*

CHORUS: The most memorable Chorus in Shakespeare is in 'Henry V' whose speeches are among the play's finest passages. If his appeal to the audience to use its imagination, after asking if 'this cockpit' can hold 'the vasty fields of France', is his most famous speech, his others are scarcely less notable, especially his word picture of the two camps the night before Agincourt. *Henry V.* There are also two Chorus speeches in *Romeo and Juliet* before Acts I and II; a PROLOGUE before *Troilus and Cressida* and *Henry VIII*, which also has an EPILOGUE. (*Also see* Gower, Rumour *and* Time.)

CICERO: A Roman senator who listens to Casca's description of the portents he has seen. Described by Brutus as having ferret and fiery eyes and being a man that will 'never follow any thing that other men begin', he is not asked to join the conspiracy. We later hear of his death by order of Octavius, Antony and Lepidus. *Julius Caesar*

CIMBER, METELLUS: One of the conspirators against Caesar. He wishes to enlist Cicero, also Caius Ligarius, wanting the former because his silver hairs will enlist public support, the rest of the conspirators being youthful. In the Senate, his suit to have his brother's banishment repealed signals the moment for the assassination. *Julius Caesar*

CINNA: One of the conspirators whose job it is to throw letters through Brutus's window allegedly written by Romans who fear Caesar's ambition. After the assassination he disappears from the play. *Julius Caesar*

CINNA THE POET: He is attacked by a mob when on his way to Caesar's funeral, being mistaken for Cinna the conspirator. He is torn to pieces—'for his bad verses', says one citizen. *Julius Caesar*

CLARENCE, GEORGE, DUKE OF: He is made a duke by his brother, Edward IV, after the Battle of Towton, but, because he disapproves of the King's marriage to Lady Grey, he deserts with Warwick to the Lancastrians. Later, he changes sides again, and at Tewkesbury he is one of the murderers of Henry VI's son, Prince Edward. *3 Henry VI*

He is now a major obstacle in the path of his brother Gloucester to the throne. Edward IV imprisons him because of a prophecy that his children will be killed by a man whose name begins with G. In the Tower, Richard has him murdered, but not before he has told the governor, Brakenbury, of a dream he has had, in one of the great speeches of the play, after which two murderers take over. They deal with 'false, fleeting, perjur'd Clarence' in a grippingly melodramatic scene. *Richard III*

CLARENCE, THOMAS, DUKE OF: The King's second son. Henry asks him to help Prince Hal. *2 Henry IV*

He has a non-speaking rôle in the last scene. *Henry V*

CLAUDIO: A young gentleman of Vienna and the brother of Isabella. Under a newly-enforced immorality law, he is condemned to die by the Duke's Deputy, Angelo, for seducing Juliet who is now pregnant. Isabella tells him that he will be spared if she gives herself to Angelo. He agrees with her that such an exchange is unthinkable, but the thought of death—'Ay, but to die, and go we know not where; to lie in cold obstruction and to rot'—changes him into what Isabella calls a 'faithless coward', as he urges her to give in to Angelo. He repents his cowardice, but Angelo, though he is tricked into thinking that Isabella has given herself to him, still orders his execution. The provost does not carry out his orders, and when Angelo's crimes are exposed, Claudio, now freed, is ordered to marry Juliet by the Duke. *Measure for Measure*

A young Florentine lord in Duke Pedro's service. Having done 'the feats of a lion' in the wars, he is now in love with Hero. His inexperience and suspicious nature trigger off the main plot of the play. The evil Don John, jealous of Claudio, arranges that Claudio and Don Pedro shall apparently see Hero allowing one of John's followers, Borachio, make love to her: actually it is one of Hero's women. At the church the next day Claudio publicly and savagely denounces Hero who, it is later given out, is dead. Claudio learns the truth about John's deception, but not that Hero is still alive. He tells Hero's father, Leonato, that he will marry his niece, and discovers that she is none other than Hero herself. As Claudio's lack of knowledge of women, impetuosity, naïvety and obsession with Honour are so amply demonstrated, one can only hope he and Hero will be happy. *Much Ado About Nothing*

CLAUDIUS: King of Denmark after murdering his brother, the father of Prince Hamlet, and marrying Gertrude, Hamlet's mother. A convincing villain, we meet him thanking his Court for an easy transfer of power. He asks Hamlet why 'the clouds still hang' on him and begs him to stay at Elsinore, not return to school. Not knowing that the Ghost has told Hamlet how he was murdered, Claudius sends two of his school-friends, Rosencrantz and Guildenstern, to spy on him. Polonius, his Lord Chamberlain, tells him Hamlet is mad for his daughter, Ophelia's, love, but, after the two watch Hamlet and Ophelia, Claudius decides his behaviour is more dangerous than love and that Hamlet must be sent to England.

He watches a play staged at Hamlet's request, which follows the story of how he murdered Hamlet's father, and he guiltily stops the performance. He tries to pray and Hamlet fails to take the opportunity to kill him. After Hamlet kills Polonius, Claudius sends him to England with Rosencrantz and Guildenstern. They do not know that they carry orders from Claudius that Hamlet is to be killed on arrival.

While Claudius watches the mad Ophelia, her brother, Laertes, breaks in. Hamlet's safe return is imminent, and Claudius and Laertes, frantic with grief because Ophelia has now drowned herself, plot a duel in which Hamlet will be 'accidentally' killed with a poisoned foil. But Laertes is mortally wounded and confesses his guilt. Hamlet stabs Claudius and forces him to drink poison.

Claudius is a sensual, ambitious, smooth scoundrel, who loves his wife, shows his guilt by heavy drinking and is capable of real remorse. *Hamlet*

CLAUDIUS AND VARRO: Servants of Brutus who sleep in his tent the night before the battle of Philippi. *Julius Caesar*

CLEOMENES: A lord of Sicilia who is sent to the oracle of Apollo at Delphi by Leontes to find out if his wife, Hermione, is chaste. He returns with the message that she is. Sixteen years later he tells Leontes that he has done penance enough. *The Winter's Tale*

CLEON: The Governor of Tarsus and husband of the evil Dionyza. Pericles arrives with corn that helps his country in famine, and Cleon gratefully agrees to bring up Pericles' infant daughter Marina. Later, when Dionyza, jealous for her own daughter, plots to murder Marina, Cleon is shocked, but conceals her crime (which fortunately misfires) and makes Pericles believe that Marina has died from natural causes. *Pericles*

CLEOPATRA: The play's famous heroine, whom so few actresses have managed to portray convincingly, not least because Enobarbus's great speech about her and her 'infinite variety' makes audiences expect a veritable goddess of love.

This 'lass unparallel'd', as Charmian says of her after her death, is endlessly fascinating, frank, brilliant, amusing, sensual, hot-tempered and capricious to a degree. In the first scene the grand passion is at its height, with an undertow of criticism from one of Antony's men about his 'cooling a gypsy's lust'. Antony is forced to go to Rome. She sends daily messages to her 'man of men' and when a messenger tells her he has married Octavia, she nearly kills him. She later demands to know what her rival is like and transforms the facts that Octavia is less tall than she is and low-voiced, into 'dull of tongue and dwarfish'.

Antony returns, with Octavius Caesar following to crush them both. She wrongly advises a sea battle, but at Actium her fleet flees. The shamed Antony upbraids her, but they are reconciled. He again reviles her when she receives a messenger from Caesar, but again they are reconciled. They are finally defeated and this time his rage is so terrible that she flees to her Monument, sending him a message that she has killed herself. He is carried to her after mortally wounding himself and dies in her arms. She learns that Caesar is going to display her in triumph in Rome, so puts on her finest robes, places an asp on her breast and dies quietly after a matchless series of speeches about Antony. Their magnificence has never been surpassed, or even approached except, perhaps, by Wagner when he came to compose Isolde's *Liebestod* (love death). Both heroines welcome death. It will redeem them and they will be reunited with their lovers. *Antony and Cleopatra*

CLERK OF CHATHAM: The rebel, Jack Cade, has him hanged for being able to read and count. *2 Henry VI*

CLIFFORD, LORD: A supporter of Henry VI. With Buckingham, he persuades Cade's followers to abandon him. He is later killed by York at St. Albans. *2 Henry VI*

CLIFFORD, LORD (YOUNG CLIFFORD): The son of the above who sees him killed at St. Albans. After a moving lament over his body, he escapes. *2 Henry VI*. He has his revenge by killing first Rutland, York's son, then York himself. At Towton it is his turn to die. *3 Henry VI*

CLITUS: A servant of Brutus, who, after his defeat at Philippi, urges Clitus to kill him. 'I'll rather kill myself,' says Clitus. He runs off as Antony and Octavius approach, urging his master to fly too. *Julius Caesar*

CLOTEN: The King's stepson. Brutish, foolish, bullying, lecherous and cowardly, he is beside himself that his beloved Imogen had married Posthumus, a mere gentleman, but even when he has 'assail'd her with musics' at his mother's instructions, he is stung to hear her say that she loves the 'meanest garment' of her banished husband, Posthumus, more than him. When he hears that Imogen has fled to Milford Haven to find Posthumus, he gets hold of a suit of the exile's clothes, dresses in them, and sets out to kill him in front of Imogen, then ravish her. But he is killed by Guiderius, who cuts off his head. Curiously, this despicable character earlier shows some real spirit when speaking to Caius Lucius, the Roman Ambassador, for he suddenly becomes a British patriot. *Cymbeline*

CLOWN: An unnamed Clown has a small scene with some musicians in Cyprus and one with Desdemona. *Othello*.

The Old Shepherd's Son is another unnamed Clown. He buries what is left of Antigonus after his encounter with a bear; he kindly helps Autolycus who alleges he has been robbed, and has his pockets picked for his pains; he buys ballads for Mopsa and Dorcas; he tells his father to tell Leontes how Perdita was found in Bohemia, and, when he is made a gentleman, he decides to live up to it by swearing and lying. A very good-natured, happy character. *The Winter's Tale*

40

A Clown brings Cleopatra asps in a basket. *Antony and Cleopatra*

A Clown brings in a basket with two pigeons in it to Titus. *Titus Andronicus*

Other Clowns are named. *Also see* Fool

COBWEB: One of Titania's fairies. Bottom promises to 'make bold with' him if he should cut his finger and later commissions him to kill a bee and bring its honey-bag to him. *A Midsummer Night's Dream*

COLEVILE, SIR JOHN: An opponent of the King and, according to John of Lancaster, a famous rebel. Yet he surrenders to Falstaff without a fight. Lancaster sends him to be executed in York. *2 Henry IV*

COMINIUS: A Consul and the commander of the Roman army which defeats the Volscians and captures Corioli. He names Caius Marcius 'Coriolanus' for his bravery in the campaign. Later, he tries to prevent Coriolanus's banishment from Rome and warns his fellow Romans of the danger they are in when Coriolanus allies himself with his former Volscian enemies. He tries to prevent him attacking Rome. *Coriolanus*

CONRADE: A follower of the vengeful Don John. He and Borachio both promise to help John deceive Claudio into thinking Hero is faithless, but he is not there when the deception takes place. While Borachio is telling him about it, they are both arrested by the Watch. When Dogberry calls him a naughty varlet, Conrade tells him he is an ass. *Much Ado About Nothing*

CONSPIRATORS: They plot with Aufidius and, with him, kill Coriolanus. *Coriolanus*

CONSTABLE OF FRANCE: He warns the Dauphin that Henry V is no longer the shallow youth he was, but he urges an attack on the English, being only sorry that their numbers are so few. He is in a boastful mood at Agincourt, but, before he is killed, realizes that the French have been utterly defeated. *Henry V*

CONSTANCE: The mother of Arthur, whom she is determined to see on the throne. France and Austria support her claim and she is in despair when they temporarily make peace with John. When he later defeats them and captures Arthur she goes mad. Passionate, grief-stricken, scornful and tender in her love for her son, she is also very voluble and even her friends comment on this. 'Her presence would have interrupted much,' says the French King at one point, and John hopes to 'stop her exclamation'. But Shakespeare does not question her sincerity even though he mocks her a little. She is later reported dead. *King John*

CORDELIA: King Lear's youngest daughter. When he decides to divide his kingdom between his daughters, he disinherits her because, unlike her false sisters, Goneril and Regan, she cannot bring herself publicly to declare her love for him. 'My love's more richer than my tongue,' she says to herself. She merely loves Lear, she says, 'according to my bond'.
At once, one of her suitors, Burgundy, scuttles away, but the King of France asks to marry her: she is 'most rich, being poor'. They leave and Cordelia does not return until much later when she and her husband invade Britain to avenge Lear's wrongs. There is a touching reunion, but Cordelia's forces are defeated and she and Lear are captured. She is hanged, her reprieve coming too late. Lear brings in her body, then dies himself.
Cordelia is a short part, but a memorable and touching one. Freud called her the embodiment of the death wish, which shows that he could write rubbish as well as the next man. *King Lear*

CORIN: A kindly, old shepherd who arranges to buy his churlish master's house, flocks and land for Rosalind and Celia. He holds his own in conversation with Touchstone, who tells him he is damned for not having been at court, and he has a classic short speech in praise of his life as a true labourer which ends with 'and the greatest of my pride is to see my ewes graze and my lambs suck'. *As You Like It*

CORIOLANUS (CAIUS MARCIUS): A Roman general and flawed hero. A brilliant warrior, his pride is his downfall. He despises his soldiers and the people of Rome and their tribunes, and patience and self-control are unknown to him. When Aufidius calls him 'Thou boy of tears', the taunt against his immaturity is just. Yet many of his searing jibes at his enemies, especially the tribunes, are fair ones. Any production which does not partly let us respect the hero and allow him some nobility is untrue to the play.

Caius Marcius, 'chief enemy of the people', is deeply unpopular despite his services to Rome: a citizen says his deeds were all done for pride and to please his mother, Volumnia. A famine is blamed on the patricians but mainly on him. He curses them for their inconsistency, then goes to fight the Volscians. He takes Corioli and is rewarded with the name Coriolanus, but he has treated his soldiers badly and incurred the enmity of the Volscian, Tullus Aufidius.

The Senate wants him as consul, but he finds it too humiliating to beg for votes. He is elected but the tribunes inflame opinion against him, claiming he refused the people free grain. He says they do not deserve it because they would not fight. His death is demanded. When he speaks to the people at his domineering mother's request, he explodes in wrath and is banished. After a painful family farewell, he goes to Antium and offers himself to Aufidius as an ally. They march on frightened Rome and only the pleas of his mother, wife and child stop him taking the city. Now Aufidius is furious with him for his popularity with the Volscians and his refusal to take Rome. He and some conspirators rouse the people of Antium against Coriolanus, who is murdered. *Coriolanus*

CORNELIUS: A doctor. Cymbeline's queen, wishing to kill her stepdaughter, Imogen, asks him for poison. He gives her instead a drug which makes a 'show of death'. At the end he tells Cymbeline of the Queen's deathbed confession. *Cymbeline*

He and VOLTIMAND are sent by Claudius to the 'impotent and bed-rid' King of Norway to try and stop his nephew Fortinbras's invasion of Denmark. They are successful, as Voltimand later reports. *Hamlet*

CORNWALL, DUKE OF: The well-matched husband of the evil Regan. He has Kent, acting as Lear's messenger, put in the stocks and commands Gloucester to shut his doors on Lear, leaving the old man to the mercy of the storm. He puts out Gloucester's eyes for helping Lear—'out, vile jelly!'—but is killed by one of his own servants who cannot endure his cruelty. *King Lear*

COSTARD: A clown who breaks the King of Navarre's order that no woman shall come within a mile of his court by consorting with the 'country wench' Jaquenetta. He is put in the custody of Don Armado, his rival for the wench. The Don releases him to carry a letter to Jaquenetta and he is also given a letter by Berowne to be taken to Rosaline. The letters are wrongly delivered amid much merriment. In the performance of the 'Nine Worthies' he plays Pompey the Great, surviving the rude barracking of his betters. *Love's Labour's Lost*

COURT, ALEXANDER: The least vocal of the soldiers who talk on the night before Agincourt and are joined by the King. *Henry V*

COURTEZAN: A woman who confuses Antipholus of Syracuse with his twin, Antipholus of Ephesus, and asks the wrong one for a chain he promised to give her and a ring he took at dinner with her. She later tells the Duke of Ephesus about the ring, so incriminating the wrong Antipholus. *The Comedy of Errors*

CRAB: Launce's dog and a splendid 'straight man' in several of the clown's scenes, being memorably insulted by his master. *The Two Gentlemen of Verona*

CRANMER, THOMAS: The Archbishop of Canterbury. He is an observer at the divorce trial, and crowns Anne Bullen off-stage. In the last act he defends himself against his enemies to Henry, who remains his loyal friend when he is accused of heresy by Gardiner. The King tells him he must be godfather to the infant Elizabeth and, at her christening, Cranmer speaks prophetically about the glories in store for Elizabeth and her fortunate people. *Henry VIII*

CRESSIDA: The daughter of Calchas. Her father having gone over to the Greeks, she lives with Pandarus who acts as go-between for her and her beloved Troilus. When the two finally meet she swears to be true to him or else let 'false maids in love' be dubbed 'As false as Cressid'. But she is exchanged for the captured Antenor because of her father's services to the Greeks and, for all her fond fare-wells to Troilus, at once proves a born flirt, to put it mildly. As Ulysses comments: 'Her wanton spirits look out At every joint and motive of her body.' Troilus, though warned by Ulysses, has the misfortune to watch her betraying him with Diomedes. Shakespeare draws her very convincingly as a sensuous girl, by no means corrupt, but, unlike Troilus, incapable of being faithful for any length of time to a single person. *Troilus and Cressida*

CROMWELL, THOMAS: He is little more than Wolsey's henchman, being tearfully present when his master laments his fall from power. Lovell notes his growing power in the last act. *Henry VIII*

CUPID: A character in a masque at Timon's house, who praises his generosity. *Timon of Athens*

CURAN: A courtier who tells Edmund that the Dukes of Albany and Cornwall have fallen out, also that Cornwall and his wife, Regan, will be arriving at Gloucester's castle that night. *King Lear*

CURIO: One of Orsino's gentlemen. *Twelfth Night*

CURTIS: A servant of Petruchio's at his country house. He

is interested to hear from Grumio whether Katharine is 'so hot a shrew as she's reported?' *The Taming of the Shrew*

CYMBELINE: King of Britain. Though the play is named after him, he is a comparatively minor character. We meet him after he has married a second wife who hates him and wants the throne for her brutish son, Cloten. He exiles his daughter, Imogen, for marrying Posthumus, a poor, though honourable, man, but he is a patriot, and, when the Roman ambassador arrives demanding tribute, he refuses and finds his kingdom invaded by the Romans. His troops are victorious, thanks to the action of Belarius, whom he has banished long ago and who has kidnapped his two sons and brought them up in the wilds. One of them has killed Cloten and Cymbeline has him arrested, though by now he realizes his queen's villainy. Belarius tells him the truth about his own and the boys' identity and all ends happily, with the King agreeing to go on paying tribute to Rome for the sake of peace and friendship. The elderly and feeble king is no great part. *Cymbeline*

D

DANCER: Speaker of the Epilogue. *2 Henry IV*

DARDANIUS: One of Brutus's servants. Brutus asks him to kill him after his defeat at Philippi. He refuses and flees at the approach of Antony and Octavius. *Julius Caesar*

DAUPHIN: *see* Charles *and* Lewis

DAUGHTER OF ANTIOCHUS, THE: The daughter of the King of Antioch and his incestuous lover. A great beauty, she has many suitors despite the fact that all who wish to marry her must answer a riddle or die. Pericles answers it, thereby finding out about the incest, and has to flee for his life. Later, the King and his daughter are 'shrivell'd up' by a 'fire from heaven'. *Pericles*

DAVY: Justice Shallow's servant who runs his estate. He talks his master out of taking action against William Visor of Woncot, despite the fact that the man is a knave, by improbably reasoning that a knave cannot speak for himself, unlike an honest man. Old Shallow is satisfied. *2 Henry IV*

DECIUS BRUTUS: *see* Brutus, Decius

DEIPHOBUS: A son of Priam. *Troilus and Cressida*

DEMETRIUS: A friend of Antony's who only appears in the opening scene. *Antony and Cleopatra*

One of the four lovers, less bold and more the rejected swain than his counterpart, Lysander, but not so very different from him. Hermia rejects him, though her father prefers him to Lysander. When he hears from Helena that the pair have fled from Athens to the woods, he pursues them. There, Oberon uses his magic to make him fall in love with Helena. He and Lysander agree to fight over Helena, but Puck, on Oberon's orders, makes them fall asleep. In the end he is paired with Helena who has loved him all along. *A Midsummer Night's Dream*

See Chiron *and* Demetrius. *Titus Andronicus*

DENNIS: He has a minute part as Oliver's servant. *As You Like It*

DENNY, SIR ANTONY: He brings Cranmer to the King in the last act. *Henry VIII*

DERBY, THOMAS STANLEY: *See* Stanley

DERCETAS: One of Antony's friends. After Antony falls on his sword, Dercetas takes it to Caesar and offers to serve him. *Antony and Cleopatra*

DESDEMONA: The wife of Othello and the noble heroine of the play. The daughter of a Venetian Senator, Brabantio, she falls in love with Othello the Moor and marries him

47

secretly. Her first appearance in the play is in the Council Chamber after Othello has described how he won her. Her father reluctantly relents and she asks to be allowed to go with her husband to Cyprus. 'Honest' Iago is asked by Othello to escort her.

They arrive before Othello, and Iago, noting her friendly relationship with Othello's lieutenant, Cassio, who has been promoted over him, re-states a plan he has uttered earlier, that he will arouse Othello's jealousy by suggesting that their friendship is something more. Iago has Cassio disgraced and the latter asks Desdemona to intercede for him with Othello. From that moment she is doomed. Accidentally dropping a handkerchief Othello gave her, it is taken by Iago from his wife, Emilia, and used to make Othello even more jealous. In scene after scene Othello's treatment of Desdemona becomes more brutal, and, finally, he kills her. With her dying breath she refuses to betray her murderer, saying to Emilia, 'Commend me to my kind Lord.'

For all her innocence, Desdemona has great character and strength. Though utterly baffled and hurt by Othello's savage attacks, she unsentimentally tries to defend herself. She is bemused enough to make things worse by bringing up the subject of Cassio at the most unfortunate moments. Dignified, devoted and attractive, only very fine actresses have done her full justice. *Othello*

DIANA: The daughter of the Widow. She is pursued by Bertram and agrees to let him into her room one night, but allows her place in bed to be taken by Bertram's abandoned wife, Helena. Diana then goes to the King of France's court and claims Bertram has seduced and refused to marry her. The plot thickens enough for the King to order her to jail, but Helena, thought to be dead by Bertram, arrives with the Widow. All is explained and the King grants her a dowry for her services to Helena. In a letter she signs her name as Diana Capilet. *All's Well that Ends Well*

A goddess who visits the hero in a dream in the last act and tells him to go to the temple at Ephesus. There he finds his long-lost wife. *Pericles*

DICK: A butcher from Ashford and one of the rebel, Cade's, followers. He is not taken in by Cade's claims to aristocratic ancestry, as he shows in cynical asides, but he is fierce enough, earning a tribute from Cade: 'Thou behavedst thyself as if thou hadst been in thine own slaughter-house.' *2 Henry VI*

DIOMEDES: One of Cleopatra's servants. After the Queen has sent word to Antony that she is dead, she sends Diomedes to say that she is still alive, but by now Antony has stabbed himself and is dying. Diomedes has him brought to Cleopatra. *Antony and Cleopatra*

A Greek general sent into Troy to bring out Cressida in exchange for the captured Antenor. Troilus warns him to use her well or risk his throat being cut. Later, he has to endure the sight of Diomedes and Cressida embracing and making an assignation. The two men meet in battle, but Diomedes escapes. An outspoken character, especially in a searing denunciation to Paris of the harm Helen has caused. *Troilus and Cressida*

DION: A lord of Sicilia, sent with Cleomenes by Leontes to Apollo's temple at Delphi to find out if his wife, Hermione, is faithful. They bring back news that she is. Sixteen years later, he urges the King to remarry and produce an heir. *The Winter's Tale*

DIONYZA: The murderous wife of Cleon, governor of Ephesus, who has promised Pericles to look after his daughter, Marina. But her own daughter, Philoten, is so much less beautiful and brilliant than Marina that she arranges to have her murdered, and thinks that it has been done. She has the supposed assassin poisoned and pretends to mourn Marina—who has been seized by pirates—when Pericles comes to see her. She and her husband are burnt when their palace is set on fire by an angry mob. *Pericles*

49

DOCTOR: Part of Cordelia's retinue when she returns to Britain. He helps to tend the mad King. *King Lear*

DOCTORS: There are two doctors. One, a 'Doctor of Physic', watches Lady Macbeth sleepwalking and is, presumably, the Scottish Doctor, though not all agree. The other, the English Doctor, tells Malcolm that Macbeth is going to cure the sick by touching them and later reports to Macbeth on his wife's mental state, her 'thick-coming fancies'. *Macbeth*

DOGBERRY: The head constable of Messina and a clownish character given to malapropisms, a spectacular one being 'you shall comprehend all vagrom men'. His Watch captures Conrade and Borachio, and Leonato tells him to examine them. He does so when he has found out if 'our whole dissembly' has appeared, and, though he accuses his two captives of the wrong crimes, he brings the plot against Hero to light. He tells Leonato, and asks that when punishment is considered, it should be remembered that he has been called an ass. *Much Ado About Nothing*

DOLABELLA: A friend of Octavius Caesar, who sends him to demand Antony's surrender. He finds him already dead. He tells Cleopatra that she will be led in Caesar's triumph and warns her that she has only three days before she and her children will be sent for. This decides Cleopatra to kill herself. *Antony and Cleopatra*

DONALBAIN: King Duncan's younger son. When his father is murdered he flees to Ireland and his brother, Malcolm, to England. They are suspected of the crime. *Macbeth*

DORCAS: A shepherdess who loves the Clown. She dances in the sheep-shearing scene and sings 'Get you hence, for I must go' with Mopsa and Autolycus. *The Winter's Tale*

DORICLES: The name which Florizel calls himself. *The Winter's Tale*

DORSET, MARQUIS OF: The son of Queen Elizabeth, Edward IV's wife by her first husband. After his brother is executed, she sends him to join Richmond. *Richard III*

DOUGLAS, ARCHIBALD, EARL OF: Defeated by Hotspur and taken prisoner, but when Hotspur rebels against the King, Douglas joins him: the two men admire each other very much. Douglas fights valiantly at Shrewsbury, killing Sir Walter Blunt who is dressed like the King, as are others. Douglas, told of this, swears 'I will kill all his coats.' He finds the King who is saved by Prince Hal. When all is lost he flees and is captured. For his bravery, Hal releases him without ransom. *1 Henry IV*

DROMIO: The name of the twin slaves who serve twin masters, Antipholus of Ephesus and of Syracuse. In this comedy of mistaken identities, they add to the confusion and, unlike their masters, find themselves being beaten continually throughout the action of the play in the best farcical manner. At the end they are happily reunited. *The Comedy of Errors*

DUKE (SENIOR): Rosalind's father who has been deposed by his younger brother, Frederick, and forced to seek sanctuary in the Forest of Arden. He finds life there very pleasant, having a number of happy courtiers with him, and welcomes Orlando to his company. When everything ends happily, he promises not to forget his friends and tells everyone to enjoy the wedding festivities. An amiable figure in a golden world. *As You Like It*

DULL, ANTONY: A simple, ignorant constable who first appears after arresting Costard for breaking a royal edict by 'consorting' with a woman, Jaquenetta. Later he reappears to be upbraided by Holofernes for speaking 'no word all this while' and confesses 'Nor understood none neither, sir.' However, he agrees to 'make one in a dance' in a forthcoming entertainment, or play the tabor, if required. *Love's Labour's Lost*

DUMAIN: One of the three young lords who, with the King of Navarre, have forsworn the company of women for three years. However, he is soon in love with Katharine, his 'most divine Kate', and, though his part is less showy than Berowne's, he suddenly comes out with the delightful ode, 'On a day, alack the day!' *Love's Labour's Lost*

DUNCAN: The King of Scotland. He hears from a wounded Sergeant how Macbeth and Banquo have defeated the Norwegians and Scottish rebels and decides to make Macbeth Thane of Cawdor. His next and final scene is at Macbeth's castle, where he comes to stay, only to be murdered by Macbeth. *Macbeth*

E

EDGAR: Gloucester's legitimate son. His bastard brother, Edmund, envying his position and wanting to supplant him, persuades their father that Edgar wants to kill him. Meanwhile, he makes Edgar believe that Gloucester is after his blood. Edgar flees, disguising himself as a Tom o' Bedlam, an inmate of a lunatic asylum let out to beg money for his keep. While a storm is raging on a heath, he meets Lear, his Fool, and Kent.

Left alone, Edgar meets his blinded father and hears him regretting his treatment of his son. He guides him to Dover where Gloucester plans to hurl himself from a cliff. Edgar describes an imaginary cliff-top scene, then makes his father jump on flat ground. The old man thinks his life has been miraculously spared. Edgar saves his father's life by killing Oswald, in whose pocket there is a letter in which Goneril vows her love to Edmund. Edgar, still disguised, gives the letter to Goneril's husband, Albany, who also learns in the letter that his wife wants to be rid of him. Still in disguise, he kills his brother, but before Edmund dies he learns

Edgar's identity and that their father's heart 'burst smilingly' when told who had been his guide. Finally, Edgar is made joint ruler with Kent by Albany. *King Lear*

EDMUND: Gloucester's illegitimate son. His father has 'often blushed to acknowledge him', though he is fond enough of Edmund. But the son is proud of his bastardy and is determined to remove the obstacle of his legitimate brother, Edgar, by smearing him to his father. 'Now, gods, stand up for bastards!' he exults, and at first they seem to. He tells his father that Edgar is out to kill him and he also tells his brother that his father is swearing vengeance against him. Edgar is banished and flees. Edmund considers himself free from superstitions. He despises his father for being guided by the sun, the moon and the stars. 'Thou, Nature art my goddess,' he says, and rejoices in his villainy so engagingly that he enlists the audience's sneaking sympathy. However, by telling Cornwall that Gloucester had hoped to help Lear, he precipitates the blinding of his father by Regan and Cornwall.

He soon has Regan as his lover and Goneril in love with him and wanting to exchange him for her husband: 'To both these sisters have I sworn my love,' he confides to us, before leading troops against Lear and Cordelia. Finally, he is killed in combat with a disguised Edgar, learning who he is before he dies. In a moment of repentance he cancels the orders that Lear and Cordelia shall be killed, though it is too late. *King Lear*

EDWARD IV: He first appears as the Earl of March, York's eldest son. He and his brother Richard stand bail for York when he is arrested for treason. *2 Henry VI.* The sons urge York to seize the throne, but their father is murdered at Wakefield. Edward defeats Henry's troops at Towton and becomes King, marrying Lady Grey. He is captured but manages to escape, and wins the battles of Barnet and Tewkesbury. *3 Henry VI.* He appears briefly as a sick man and hears from Richard that Clarence, their brother has been killed though he has revoked the order. His final speech is a gloomy one, fearing God's justice. *Richard III.* He is characterized as lustful—'wanton'—but strong and ambitious.

EDWARD V: Son of the above. An infant who is kissed by Clarence and Richard. *3 Henry VI.* He and his brother are persuaded by Richard, in a chilling scene, to lodge in the Tower. He speaks up for himself, looking forward to winning France if he should grow up, but Richard has the boys murdered. *Richard III*

EDWARD, PRINCE OF WALES: The son of Henry. His father proclaims York his heir, which makes Edward protest that he cannot be disinherited. Queen Margaret agrees and when Warwick joins her, the Prince is betrothed to Warwick's daughter. At Tewkesbury, he is captured and stabbed by Edward IV, Gloucester and Clarence in front of his mother. *3 Henry VI*

EGEUS: Hermia's father, who is determined that she shall marry Demetrius and complains to Duke Theseus about her, threatening her with a nunnery or death if she does not do as he says. However, at the end of the play, Theseus makes him let her marry Lysander. *A Midsummer Night's Dream*

EGLAMOUR, SIR: A kindly gentleman who helps Silvia escape to join Valentine, her father wishing her to marry Thurio. However, when they are attacked by outlaws in a forest, he runs away. *The Two Gentlemen of Verona*

ELBOW: A constable as prone to malapropisms as Dogberry in 'Much Ado'. He arrests Pompey and Froth, 'notorious benefactors', and brings them before the deputies. He accuses Froth of abusing Mistress Elbow, his pregnant wife: he has eaten her last two prunes. *Measure for Measure*

ELINOR, QUEEN: Henry II's widow and John's mother. She is aware that John's claim to the throne is a weak one, but supports him against young Arthur's better claim. She decides that Faulconbridge is the bastard son of Richard

Cœur-de-Lion and tells him 'I am a soldier and now bound to France'. There she goes with John, who later hears of her death. An unlikable character. *King John*

ELIZABETH, QUEEN (LADY GREY): She first appears as the widow of Sir John Grey, pleading that her husband's lands be given her after he has been killed. Edward IV falls in love with her and marries her. She later appears with the infant Edward, Prince of Wales. *3 Henry VI*. She and her relations suffer Richard's insults: he has always looked down on their family. Then Edward dies. She and her younger son, Richard of York, seek sanctuary. Richard murders her brother, Lord Grey, and her sons, Edward V and Richard. Her last scene begins with her railing at Richard, but ends with her agreeing to try and persuade her daughter Elizabeth to marry him. As she goes, Richard sneers: 'Relenting fool, and shallow, changing woman.' *Richard III*

ELY, BISHOP OF: Listens to the Archbishop of Canterbury describing the King's reformation and to his plan to encourage him to invade France. *Henry V*

ELY, BISHOP OF (JOHN MORTON): Sent by Gloucester from a council meeting to get some strawberries from his garden. We later learn that he has been arrested, has escaped and fled to join Richmond. *Richard III*

EMILIA: Iago's wife and Desdemona's companion and servant. She unwittingly helps to bring about the tragedy by keeping Desdemona's dropped handkerchief instead of giving it straight back, also by helping Cassio meet her mistress. She loves her husband, who has no trouble in fooling her, for all her candour and common sense. When she finds out the truth she rails at Othello for his gullibility and at Iago for his perfidy. To silence her, he kills her. *Othello*

An attendant of Hermione's. She tells Paulina that Hermione has had a daughter in prison. *The Winter's Tale*

ENOBARBUS: Antony's closest friend. He speaks the incomparable description of how Cleopatra first met Antony, culminating in 'Age cannot wither her, nor custom stale her infinite variety . . .', addressing it to Mecaenas and Agrippa in Rome. He advises Antony against meeting Caesar in a sea battle and sees Cleopatra's fleet flee, followed by Antony's. He deserts his master, but Antony sends him all his treasure and he is so overcome with shame and remorse that he dies of a broken heart. An eloquent, witty and attractive character. *Antony and Cleopatra*

EROS: A servant of Antony, whose part, though small, is memorable. Antony orders Eros to kill him, but rather than do it, he kills himself and shows Antony how to die. *Antony and Cleopatra*

ERPINGHAM, SIR THOMAS: One of Henry's officers. On the night before Agincourt the King borrows the cloak of this 'good knight'. *Henry V*

ESCALUS: An 'ancient Lord' whom the Duke appoints to be Angelo's deputy in carrying out a reform campaign. Far more lenient than Angelo, he pleads with him to spare Claudio's life and he lets off Pompey and Froth with a mere warning. Later, he condemns the disguised Duke to prison for slandering the state. The Duke, having revealed himself, forgives the old man. *Measure for Measure*

The wise, commanding Prince of Verona who breaks up the street riot between the Capulets and Montagues and threatens them with death 'if ever you disturb our streets again'. He reappears after the deaths of Mercutio and Tybalt, and banishes Romeo. His final appearance is at the end of the play where he takes charge once again. *Romeo and Juliet*

ESCANES: A lord of Tyre where he is left as governor when Pericles and Helicanus go to Tarsus. *Pericles*

ESSEX, EARL OF: He introduces Philip and Robert Faulconbridge to the King in the opening scene. *King John*

EUPHRONIUS: The defeated Antony's ambassador to Octavius Caesar. He asks that Antony may live in Egypt, if not as 'a private man in Athens' and that Cleopatra may remain Queen. Caesar turns down both requests. Dolabella describes Euphronius as Antony's schoolmaster. *Antony and Cleopatra*

EVANS, SIR HUGH: A Welsh parson. He is challenged to a duel by Doctor Caius when the bad-tempered French physician, who hopes to marry Anne Page, finds that Evans prefers Slender as a suitor. The Host of the Garter Inn sends each of them to a different spot, then admits what he has been up to, saying that he did not want to lose his doctor or parson. The pair unite against him and cheat him of three horses. Evans joins in the plot to humiliate Falstaff and rehearses the children in their parts. He dresses as a satyr and burns the fat knight with a taper. Sir Hugh's accent is very thick: he 'makes fritters of English', says Falstaff. *The Merry Wives of Windsor*

EXETER, HENRY, DUKE OF: He appears only in the first scene as a follower of Henry's, but his conscience tells him that York is 'lawful king'. *3 Henry VI*

EXETER, DUKE OF: *see* Beaufort, Thomas

EXTON, SIR PIERS (or PIERCE): He overhears Henry IV wishing that someone would rid him of Richard, so murders him in Pomfret Castle. Henry does not thank him—'I hate the murderer, love him murdered'—and banishes him. *Richard II*

F

FABIAN: One of Olivia's servants. He appears first after the plot against her steward, Malvolio, is under way. He eagerly joins in because he has fallen out of favour with

Olivia after Malvolio has reported him for organizing a bear-baiting session on her estate. At the end Olivia orders him to read out Malvolio's plea to her from where he is imprisoned, and he confesses how he and Sir Toby have plotted against their enemy. *Twelfth Night*

FALSTAFF: The boon companion of Prince Hal. *1 and 2 Henry IV*. He is reduced from the greatest comic character in English Literature to a mere butt. *The Merry Wives of Windsor*. The audience is promised at the end of *2 Henry IV* that he will appear in *Henry V*, but Shakespeare realized that he must kill off his beloved 'plump Jack' to allow Henry, his ideal hero-king, to shine without rivals or distractions.

Falstaff is not only witty but 'the cause that wit is in other men'. We meet him planning to rob travellers at Gadshill. He, Gadshill (the character, confusingly), Bardolph and Peto carry out the robbery but are robbed by the disguised Prince and Poins soon after. He later boasts how brave he was, and when Hal tells him the truth, pretends he knew it was him all along. He marches against Hotspur with a 'ragged' army he has press-ganged 'damnably'. After his famous speech deriding honour before the Battle of Shrewsbury—the very opposite of Hotspur's romantic conception of Honour—he pretends to be dead when attacked by Douglas, then claims the credit for killing Hotspur. *1 Henry IV*

This 'huge hill of flesh', still the bawdy, boastful glutton who was once page to the Duke of Norfolk, is now even more disreputable, perhaps to prepare the way for Henry's callous rejection of him. He insults the Lord Chief Justice and defrauds Mistress Quickly, while living riotously with Doll Tearsheet. Then he goes to Gloucestershire to recruit soldiers—and borrow £1,000 from his old friend, Justice Shallow. In the ensuing campaign he actually captures a famous rebel, Colevile, who surrenders without fighting. But his luck has run out. Back in Gloucestershire, he hears that Hal is now King, hurries to London, and has his heart broken when Henry publicly disowns him—'I know thee not, old man: fall to thy prayers.' *2 Henry IV*. We hear of his death in a moving speech by Mistress Quickly. *Henry V*

In *The Merry Wives of Windsor*, written, legend has it, because Queen Elizabeth wanted to see Falstaff in love, he sends love letters to Mistress Ford and Mistress Page. But at his first rendezvous with the former, he is almost caught by Ford and escapes by hiding in a dirty linen basket which is thrown into the Thames. Next, he escapes dressed as an old woman, but is cudgelled by Ford. In Windsor Park, hoping to meet Mrs. Page, he goes dressed as Herne the Hunter, and is burned by tapers and pinched by Mistress Quickly, Pistol, Evans and a group of supposed fairies. *The Merry Wives of Windsor*

Audiences have always adored the old reprobate, though puritanical attacks on him have been made. His love of Hal is genuine. When in a mock scene in Part I he says 'Banish plump Jack and banish all the world', it turns out to be an exact prophecy, for him at least. Shakespeare's divine understanding and neutrality gave Part I two heroes, Falstaff and Hotspur and he loved both. After Hotspur's death Falstaff, the greater creation, has the field to himself. He was originally called Oldcastle until the original descendants complained, when Shakespeare switched the name to Falstaff inspired by Sir John Fastolfe (*see below*).

FANG: A sheriff's officer sent to arrest Falstaff at the request of Mistress Quickly. *2 Henry IV*

FASTOLFE, SIR JOHN: A cowardly knight, described by a messenger as deserting Talbot at Patay. He later runs away at Rouen. In Paris Talbot rips the Garter from his 'craven's leg' and Henry banishes him. The real Fastolfe had a reputation for cowardice because he did desert Talbot once, but apparently was not a coward. Shakespeare almost certainly used his name for Falstaff: Fastolfe commanded a Bardolph, owned a Boar's Head Tavern and had been in the Duke of Norfolk's service! *1 Henry VI*

FATHER THAT HAS KILLED HIS SON: He carries the
body of a boy he has killed onto the stage, then discovers
his opponent was his only son. *3 Henry VI*

FAULCONBRIDGE, LADY: The mother of Robert and
Philip Faulconbridge. The latter makes her admit that his
father was Richard I. *King John*

FAULCONBRIDGE, PHILIP (THE BASTARD): The illegitimate son of Richard I and by far the most vivid and human
character in the play, a true 'Shakespeare Man' in that the
dramatist seems to identify himself with the character as he
does with Falstaff, Hotspur, Mercutio and Hamlet. He is
witty, cynical and deeply patriotic.
He is acknowledged by Queen Elinor in the first scene
as her grandson and John knights him. He serves the King
to the end, while acting as chorus-like character, comment-
ing on the action and the 'Mad world' and 'mad kings'. No
respector of persons, he insults the Duke of Austria and
later kills him in battle. He is faithful to the unworthy John
because he is the king. After swearing allegiance to the new
young King, Henry III, Philip ends the play with the
speech: 'This England never did, nor never shall, lie at the
proud foot of a conqueror.' He has a famous speech on
Commodity (Expediency). *King John*

FAULCONBRIDGE, ROBERT: The younger, but legitimate,
son of Sir Robert Faulconbridge. John grants him his
inheritance. *King John*

FEEBLE, FRANCIS: A ladies' tailor pressed into service by
Falstaff and Shallow. 'Forcible Feeble', as Falstaff calls him,
meekly accepts his fate. *2 Henry IV*

FENTON: A 'young gentleman' who loves Anne Page,
though he admits that her money first attracted him.
Anne's father dislikes his rank and his reputation for
riotous living, so Fenton bribes the Host of the Garter Inn
with £100 to help him elope with Anne, who is also being
pursued by Slender and Dr. Caius. In Windsor Park, where

Anne plays the Queen of the Fairies in the tormenting of Falstaff, the couple slip away to get married while Fenton's rivals find themselves marrying boy fairies. The deed done, Anne's parents cheerfully accept the situation. *The Merry Wives of Windsor*

FERDINAND: The King of Navarre. He and three companions have made a vow to avoid women for three years and concentrate on study. He orders that no woman can come within a mile of them. However, like his friends, he falls in love, his choice being the Princess of France. He gives himself away to a hidden Berowne by reading out a poem about her. When she is forced to return to France, she promises to return to him if he will wait a year in seclusion for her. *Love's Labour's Lost*

The son of the King of Naples. Shipwrecked with his father and followers, he is separated from them and searches the island for them. Ariel's singing leads him to Prospero's cave where he sees and falls in love with Miranda. Her father tests him by making him a slave. He is rewarded with Miranda's hand and a masque is performed for the pair, arranged by Ariel. Prospero later restores him to his father. *The Tempest*

FESTE: Olivia's Fool who tries to prove to her the folly of mourning so much for her dead brother. Her steward, Malvolio, insults him, but Olivia supports her 'allowed fool', for which he thanks her. He takes part in the duping of Malvolio and, acting as Sir Topas, the curate, pretends that the imprisoned steward is possessed by Satan. He torments him unmercifully. For all his impudence and wisdom, Feste is not an easy part for a modern audience or for an actor, but he can make a great effect, partly because he has to sing the haunting songs, 'O mistress mine', 'Come away death' and 'When that I was and a little tiny boy'. *Twelfth Night*

FIDELE: The name that Imogen adopts when she disguises herself as a boy. *Cymbeline*

FITZWATER, LORD: He accuses Aumerle of Gloucester's murder. *Richard II*

FLAMINIUS: A servant of Timon sent to borrow money from Lucullus, who offers him a bribe to pretend he has not seen him. Flaminius throws it back at him. *Timon of Athens*

FLAVIUS: Timon's faithful steward who, having tried to curb his master's disastrous generosity, helps the other servants from his own pocket after Timon's downfall. When he visits Timon in his cave, he is the only person the misanthropic hermit does not revile. *Timon of Athens*

FLAVIUS AND MARULLUS: Tribunes who appear at the start and memorably upbraid the citizens of Rome for forgetting Pompey. The two fear the growing power of Caesar. Marullus recalls when the fickle populace waited all day to 'see great Pompey pass the streets of Rome' and urges them to pray to the gods to forgive their ingratitude. Casca later says that the pair have been 'put to silence' for pulling scarfs off Caesar's images. *Julius Caesar*

FLEANCE: Banquo's son. Macbeth orders both of them killed to thwart the Witches' prophecy that Banquo shall beget a line of kings, but Fleance escapes. *Macbeth*

FLORENCE, DUKE OF: He has two scenes, in the first justifying his war against Siena, in the second making Bertram his cavalry leader. *All's Well that Ends Well*

FLORIZEL: The attractive son of King Polixenes of Bohemia. Pretending to be the humbly born Doricles, he loves Perdita, apparently a shepherd's daughter, actually the abandoned child of Leontes of Sicilia, who, years before, accused Polixenes of being his wife's lover. Polixenes is now furious at a match between a prince and a shepherdess and threatens to disinherit Florizel and kill Perdita. The lovers flee to Sicilia, pursued by Polixenes, but all ends happily. Florizel has some magnificent romantic verse in praise of Perdita. *The Winter's Tale*

FLUELLEN: A Welsh officer, able and well read in military history, but humourless and quarrelsome. We meet him driving Pistol and the Boy through the breach at Harfleur. He falls out with the Irish Captain Macmorris and with Pistol, who later has to eat a leek for insulting the Welsh. The King gives Pistol Williams' glove to wear in his cap and this leads to another quarrel. But Henry has a high regard for this fire-eater, who considers the King a true Welshman. *Henry V*

FLUTE, FRANCIS: An Athenian bellows-mender. He is given the part of Thisbe and thinks it a wandering Knight. He is shaken to discover he has to play a woman, especially as he has a beard coming. Quince says he can wear a mask. In the event, he does well and provides much amusement. *A Midsummer Night's Dream*

FOOL: He is both jester and commentator on the tragedy. He realizes the blunder Lear has made in disinheriting Cordelia, to whom he is devoted, as he is to his master. His extraordinary dialogue with its riddles, morbid jokes, songs, proverbs and insight, has made some claim that he is simple-minded. Actually, as he tries to ward off Lear's madness, he seems as sensible as he is melancholy. This haunting character disappears in the middle of the play, some believe because the original Fool may also have played Cordelia, who is absent in the middle. This may explain a startling line of Lear's near the end: 'And my poor fool is hanged.' *King Lear*

The servant of a courtesan. He has a short, ribald scene with Apemantus and servants of Timon's creditors. *Timon of Athens*

FORD, MASTER FRANK: A gentleman of Windsor. Pistol warns him that Falstaff is pursuing his wife and he jealously decides to find out if she is faithful. He disguises himself as Master Brook and, telling Falstaff he loves

Mistress Ford, asks him to woo her for him—for a bag of money. Falstaff tells him he already has an assignation with her and that Ford will soon be a cuckold. The enraged husband swears he will prevent the encounter. He arrives with friends to do so, but Falstaff has taken refuge in a laundry basket and poor Ford is mocked for his jealousy. The process is repeated, but this time Mrs. Ford lets her frantic husband into the secret that Falstaff is being duped. He apologizes to her and joins in the final humiliation of Falstaff in Windsor Park. *The Merry Wives of Windsor*

FORD, MISTRESS: A merry, but faithful, wife. Receiving a love letter from Falstaff, and finding Mistress Page has had a similar one, they plot their revenge, though her task is complicated, as told above, by her husband's jealousy. *The Merry Wives of Windsor*

FORTINBRAS: The nephew of 'old Fortinbras', King of Norway. He is about to invade Denmark to recover lost lands, but Claudius prevents this and lets him march through Denmark to attack Poland. We meet him on his way to Poland where Hamlet encounters his army. Later, as Hamlet is dying, he names Fortinbras as his successor. He arrives just after Hamlet has died, having conquered Poland, and orders that the prince shall be given military honours. *Hamlet*

FRANCE, KING OF: An old friend of Bertram's dead father who makes the young man his ward. Apparently fatally ill, he is cured by Helena, whose reward is to be the choice of a husband. She selects her adored Bertram, who scornfully rejects her as beneath him, much to the fury of the King who orders him to marry her. Later, he suspects Bertram of killing Helena, but finally learns the complicated facts. He speaks the Epilogue. *All's Well that Ends Well*

The suitor of Cordelia. Unlike Burgundy, he does not reject her when she is disinherited. He does not appear again, though later he comes over with Cordelia and an army to help Lear. We learn that he has had to return home on business of state. *King Lear*

See also Charles *and* Philip

FRANCE, PRINCESS OF: She and her three ladies travel to Navarre on a diplomatic errand for her father just when the King of Navarre and three companions have forsworn the company of women for three years. The King rapidly falls in love with her, and she with him. On the news of her father's death, she has to return home, promising that she will marry the King at the end of a year. *Love's Labour's Lost*

FRANCIS: Drawer in the main tavern scene who is mocked by Prince Hal and Poins, the latter calling him from off-stage while the Prince questions him. Francis is reduced to calls of 'anon, anon, sir'. *1 Henry IV*

FRANCISCA: A nun who welcomes Isabella and instructs her about the order of Saint Clare. *Measure for Measure*

FRANCISCO: A soldier who only appears at the beginning, challenging Bernado on the battlements and being relieved by him. *Hamlet*

One of those shipwrecked on Prospero's island with the King of Naples. He tries to cheer him by describing how he saw his missing son riding on the backs of the waves. He appears again, but says little. *The Tempest*

FREDERICK, DUKE: He has usurped the title of his elder brother. His admiration at Orlando overthrowing his wrestler is lessened when he finds that the victor is the son of an enemy. He next banishes his niece, Rosalind. His daughter, Celia, goes with her and he believes Orlando has joined them. He orders Orlando's brother, Oliver, to find him within a year or be banished himself. However, we later hear how he has gone to the Forest of Arden to kill his brother, but has met a hermit. At once he steps down from his dukedom, restores everyone's lands and, as reported, 'hath put on a religious life'. *As You Like It*

FRIAR FRANCIS: He is about to marry Hero and Claudio when the duped bridegroom savagely accuses his bride of being unfaithful. The Friar believes she is innocent and later advises her father, Leonato, to pretend she is dead and 'change slander to remorse'. He has the pleasure of seeing her vindicated. *Much Ado About Nothing*

FRIAR JOHN: A Franciscan sent by Friar Laurence to tell Romeo in Mantua that Juliet is alive in the Capulet tomb. But he is stopped from going because the constables think he may have 'infectious pestilence'. *Romeo and Juliet*

FRIAR LAURENCE: A Franciscan. Romeo tells him that he now loves Juliet, not Rosaline and he later marries the pair, hoping that it will mend the feud between their houses. He comforts Romeo after his banishment and angrily stops him killing himself, but his well-meaning plans to help the pair go disastrously astray. He gives Juliet a drug to make her appear dead, but Romeo hears that she is dead, returns from Mantua to the Capulets' tomb and poisons himself. Juliet wakes and kills herself. It is left to the kindly friar to find Romeo dead, to fail to prevent Juliet's death, then to explain to the Prince what has happened. 'I will be brief,' he says, but he is not. A delightful character, if well played. *Romeo and Juliet*

FRIAR LODOWICK: The name the Duke takes when he disguises himself as a monk. *Measure for Measure*

FRIAR PETER: He helps the Duke expose the wickedness of Angelo. *Measure for Measure*

FRIAR THOMAS: He is asked by the Duke to help him disguise himself as a friar so that he can observe his deputy, Angelo's, behaviour. *Measure for Measure*

FROTH: A foolish gentleman who is brought, with Pompey the Bawd, before the deputies by Elbow, who claims he has abused Mrs. Elbow. He is dismissed with a caution. *Measure for Measure*

G

GADSHILL: With Falstaff, Bardolph and Peto he helps rob travellers at Gadshill (confusingly). He finds out when the travellers will be leaving their inn, and after taking part in the robbery, is robbed with the rest by the disguised Prince Hal and Poins. He later encourages Falstaff to explain away their mishap with a welter of lies when they all meet at the Boar's Head Tavern. *1 Henry IV*

GALLUS: A friend of Octavius Caesar. He is one of those sent to capture Cleopatra in her monument. When she is taken, he orders her to be guarded and goes to fetch Octavius. *Antony and Cleopatra*

GANYMEDE: The name that Rosalind adopts when she disguises herself as a boy. *As You Like It*

GARDENER: He compares the state of England unfavourably to the state of his garden. *Richard II*

GARDINER: The Bishop of Winchester who, thanks to Wolsey, is made Henry's secretary. When he becomes bishop, he leads a conspiracy against Cranmer, but the King supports the man whom Gardiner calls an arch heretic and makes the pair embrace. Henry accuses Gardiner of having a 'cruel nature and a bloody'. *Henry VIII*

GARGRAVE, SIR THOMAS: An English officer killed at Orleans by a cannon shot. *1 Henry VI*

GENERAL OF THE FRENCH FORCES: In a powerful speech he refuses to surrender Bordeaux to Talbot. *1 Henry VI*

GENTLEMAN: Various gentlemen appear in the plays, all minor characters, but some having moments of glory. The Third Gentleman in *The Winter's Tale* reports to his friends about the reunion of the two kings and of Leontes and his daughter. His description of how Perdita was suddenly overcome with emotion includes: 'she did, with an "alas!" I would fain say, bleed tears, for I am sure my heart wept blood'.

Two Gentlemen are captured by pirates, along with the Duke of Suffolk, and agree to pay ransom, and one has an appalled comment when the Duke is murdered. *2 Henry VI*

Two Gentlemen set the scene at the opening. *Cymbeline*

GEORGE (GEORGE BEVIS): One of Cade's rebels. *2 Henry VI*

GERTRUDE: Hamlet's mother, the widow of the murdered king and now the wife of his murderer, King Claudius. She cares deeply for her son, and seems not to have known that Claudius killed her first husband. The Ghost tells Hamlet of her adultery with Claudius, but urges him to leave her punishment to heaven.

In the great scene with Hamlet in her apartment, he denounces her so fiercely that she cries for help. Polonius appears from his hiding-place and Hamlet kills him. He renews his attacks on her until the Ghost, unseen by her, arrives to remind him of his 'almost blunted purpose'. She thinks Hamlet is mad, but he tells her he is mad 'in craft'. She is utterly and emotionally crushed, and believes he is truly mad. The King later tells Laertes that he cannot punish Hamlet because Gertrude dotes on him, and it is she who tells Laertes that Ophelia is drowned. She dies after drinking the poisoned cup meant for Hamlet. A weak, easily dominated, sensual woman, she is by no means unsympathetic. *Hamlet*

GHOST: The ghost of Hamlet's father, King Hamlet. Before Hamlet sees him, he has twice been seen by Marcellus and Bernardo, then again by them when Horatio is with them. He tells his son to avenge him, and how he was poisoned by Claudius, but he urges Hamlet not to harm his mother, now Claudius's wife, but to leave her punishment to heaven. The Ghost appears once more to Hamlet when he is with his mother, who does not see the apparition. The appearance comes when Hamlet is heading for violence against his mother, and the Ghost urges him to remember that his task is to kill his uncle—'this visitation Is to whet thy almost blunted purpose'. Shakespeare may have played the part. *Hamlet*

GHOSTS: Apart from the Ghost in *Hamlet*, there are ghosts in four other plays.

The King's many victims appear to him in succession on the night before Bosworth, urge him to despair and die, then wish Richmond, also sleeping, victory on the morrow. *Richard III*

The Ghost of Julius Caesar appears to Brutus before the Battle of Philippi and tells him it is his evil spirit. *Julius Caesar*

The Ghost of the murdered Banquo appears to Macbeth at the banquet, making him start guiltily. *Macbeth*

Apparitions of his family appear to Posthumus, pleading to Jupiter to help him. *Cymbeline*

Fiends appear to Joan of Arc (La Pucelle). *1 Henry VI*

The spirit, Asmath, is conjured up by Margaret Jourdain and others. *2 Henry VI*

Spirits of peace appear to Queen Katharine. *Henry VIII*

The witches conjure up an armed head, a bloody child and a child crowned with a tree in its hand, eight future kings and Banquo for Macbeth's benefit. *Macbeth*

GLANSDALE, SIR WILLIAM: An officer at the siege of Orleans. *1 Henry VI*

GLENDOWER, OWEN: A Welsh rebel in one memorable scene. Before this we learn that he has defeated and captured Mortimer who has married his daughter. Both men join Hotspur's rebellion and meet him to divide up the kingdom into three parts. Hotspur enjoys teasing his Welsh ally because he believes in portents. *1 Henry IV*

GLOUCESTER, EARL OF: The father of Edgar and his illegitimate brother, Edmund. He disastrously misunderstands them and is duped by the villainous Edmund into believing that Edgar means to kill him. Edgar is forced to flee. When Lear is driven out into the storm by Regan and Cornwall, Gloucester is ordered to bar his doors to him. He disobeys, conducts Lear to a farmhouse and tells Kent to take the King to Dover. In revenge Cornwall gouges out Gloucester's eyes with Regan's encouragement and the blinded man learns that Edmund is his betrayer.

He hires the disguised Edgar to take him to Dover where he means to commit suicide from a cliff. Edgar makes him jump from flat ground and he believes himself saved by a miracle. He is reunited with Lear and, finally, with Edgar, at which point, we are told, his heart 'burst smilingly'.

Gloucester is a pathetic character. In his hour of utter despair he cries: 'Like flies to wanton boys are we to the gods. They kill us for their sport.' Gradually he recovers from this pit through Edgar's kindness. *King Lear*

GLOUCESTER, DUCHESS OF: She hopes to be queen, and hires sorcerers to foretell the future to her. She is found by York and Buckingham and banished. *2 Henry VI*

Her husband has been murdered by Mowbray at the King's command. She implores John of Gaunt, her brother-in-law, to avenge her husband, but he tells her to ask God to help her. She says she will return to her country home. *Richard II*

GLOUCESTER, HUMPHREY, DUKE OF: He has a small part attending the King, while still Prince Humphrey. *2 Henry IV*. A Duke, his part is again small, though he is continually with the King. *Henry V*. He is Protector and is incessantly quarrelling with Henry Beaufort, Bishop of Winchester. *1 Henry VI*. His wife is banished for her sorcery and he loses his position as Protector. His many enemies have him murdered (off-stage). *2 Henry VI*

GLOUCESTER, RICHARD, DUKE OF: *see* Richard III

GOBBO, LAUNCELOT: A clown in Shylock's service. He decides to leave Shylock for Bassanio. He helps Lorenzo elope with Jessica and goes to Belmont with Bassanio, after which he acts as a comic messenger. *The Merchant of Venice*

GOBBO, OLD: Launcelot's nearly blind father. He gives Bassanio a dish of doves meant for Shylock and asks that he take his son into his service. *The Merchant of Venice*

GONERIL: Lear's eldest daughter. When he divides his kingdom she vies with her sister, Regan, in hypocritically proclaiming her love for him. Cordelia, who refuses to proclaim her love publicly is disinherited. Soon the real Goneril is shown to Lear when he stays with her: even her steward Oswald is encouraged to insult him, and she complains of his followers, as she does again later with Regan. She is married to Albany whom she despises, and is unfaithful to him with Edmund, also, probably, with Oswald. She wishes to be rid of her husband and finally kills Regan, then herself. If anything, Goneril is fiercer than her tigerish sister. *King Lear*

GONZALO: An 'honest old' counsellor of Alonso, the King of Naples, who has usurped the throne from Prospero. Before the play he has provisioned the boat, into which Prospero and Miranda were put, with food, clothes and books. For all his goodness, he is more than a match for the taunts of Sebastian and Antonio on the island, and when, with the rest, he falls into Prospero's power, he is called 'My true preserver' and commended for loyally serving his present master. *The Tempest*

GOVERNOR OF HARFLEUR: He surrenders his city to Henry, having received no help from the Dauphin. *Henry V*

GOWER: He is the Chorus, Shakespeare using the actual character of the English poet, John Gower (1325–1408), from one of whose works he drew part of the plot. Gower summarizes the action and spans the years before each act and elsewhere. *Pericles*. It cannot be proved that the

Thomas Gower of *2 Henry IV* and *Henry V* is also the poet. After a brief appearance in the former, he has a number of scenes with Fluellen, where he tries to act as a brake on the Welshman's ferocious temper.

GRANDPRÉ: A French leader at Agincourt where he is killed. On the morning of the battle he describes the ragged state of the English and urges his comrades not to delay attacking them. *Henry V*

GRATIANO: A friend of Antonio and Bassanio. The latter says that he 'speaks an infinite deal of nothing' and also that he is 'too wild, too rude and bold of voice'. After promising to behave himself, he goes to Belmont with Bassanio where he marries Portia's waiting-maid, Nerissa. After Antonio's trial, Bassanio and Gratiano give up their rings to Portia and Nerissa, disguised as a lawyer and lawyer's clerk, as a requested reward for Antonio's acquittal. They are later teased for unfaithfulness. *The Merchant of Venice*

Desdemona's uncle and Brabantio's brother. In Cyprus he helps Cassio when he is attacked by Roderigo and appears later when Emilia shouts that Othello has killed Desdemona. He announces that her father is dead. Events are too much for him. *Othello*

GRAVEDIGGERS, FIRST AND SECOND: These clowns have a memorable scene in which, after conversing together, the Second Gravedigger leaves. The First discusses the skull of Yorick, the Court Jester, with Hamlet and Horatio. His 'earthy' humour is an admirable counterpoint to the grim tragedy about to reach its climax. *Hamlet*

GREEN: He, Bushy and Bagot, all favourites of the King, are described by Bolingbroke as 'The caterpillars of the commonwealth'. With Bushy he flees to Bristol, but is captured and executed. *Richard II*

GREGORY: One of Capulet's servants. At the start, he and Sampson pick a quarrel with Abraham and Balthasar, both Montagues. *Romeo and Juliet*

GREMIO: A suitor of Bianca, Katharina's sister. He hires his rival, Lucentio, as Bianca's tutor and so loses her to him. In a splendid speech, he describes the wedding of Petruchio and Katharina, revealing how the bride was kissed with 'such a clamorous smack That at the parting all the church did echo.' *The Taming of the Shrew*

GREY, LADY: *see* Elizabeth, Queen

GREY, LORD: The younger son of Elizabeth, Edward IV's wife, by her former husband. With his uncle, Rivers, he is imprisoned by order of Richard at Pomfret and executed. He calls his executioners 'damned blood-suckers'. *Richard III*

GREY, SIR THOMAS: He, Cambridge and Scroop have plotted to kill the King at Southampton but are discovered and executed. *Henry V*

GRIFFITH: A gentleman-usher to Queen Katharine who describes the death of Wolsey to the Queen when she is dying herself. *Henry VIII*

GRUMIO: One of Petruchio's servants. He sticks up for himself even when his master wrings his ears, and has one splendid scene where he describes to another servant, Curtis, the misfortunes of Katharina's trip from Padua with Petruchio. At one point the Shrew, having fallen in the mire, had come to rescue Grumio while he was being beaten by his master. *The Taming of the Shrew*

GUIDERIUS: *see* Arviragus

GUILDENSTERN: He and Rosencrantz are school friends of the Prince, who are brought to Court by Claudius to spy on Hamlet. There is no evidence of them being treacherous to him: they are simply bewildered. After Hamlet has killed Polonius he is sent to England guarded by the pair, who carry sealed orders that he shall be killed there. Hamlet changes their names for his and later hears that they have been killed. They are not strongly characterized. *Hamlet*

GUILDFORD, SIR HENRY: He welcomes guests on Wolsey's behalf to a feast at York Place. *Henry VIII*

GURNEY, JAMES: Lady Faulconbridge's servant. *King John*

H

HABERDASHER: He is made to torment Katharina by Petruchio, who has him show her a fine hat which Petruchio calls 'lewd and filthy' etc. and refuses to allow her to have it. *The Taming of the Shrew*

HAL, PRINCE: *see* Henry V

HAMLET: The Prince of Denmark and hero of Shakespeare's most famous play, and the most discussed character in all drama and, indeed, literature.

In his first scene his melancholy is commented on by his mother, Gertrude, and his uncle, Claudius, who has married her soon after the death of her husband, Hamlet's father. In a soliloquy, his sorrow, despair and rage against his mother's remarriage expose his true feelings. His friend Horatio tells him how he and others have seen the Ghost of his father on the battlements and he says he will watch for it. The Ghost tells him how he was murdered by Claudius, but that his mother is innocent of murder, if not of 'damn'd incest', and it demands revenge.

But Hamlet hesitates to act, partly from his nature, partly because he cannot be sure if he has seen an honest Ghost. He pretends to be mad and alarms Ophelia whom he loves. He arranges for a troupe of players to perform a piece very similar in plot to the way his father was killed, so that he can watch Claudius. He meets Ophelia again and terrifies her with his attacks on women and marriage. His play scheme works, the King showing his guilt. Hamlet goes to see his mother, failing to kill Claudius, whom he finds on his knees. He savagely abuses his mother and, hearing a movement behind a curtain, stabs Polonius, Ophelia's father. The Ghost appears and urges him to act, but his mother, not seeing it, is sure he is mad.

Claudius sends him to England with two friends, Rosencrantz and Guildenstern, who carry sealed orders to have him killed there. He switches the orders and sends them to die, returning home thanks to pirates that attack his ship. In a graveyard, he learns that Ophelia has drowned herself, and he wrestles in her grave with her frantic brother, Laertes. Claudius and Gertrude explain he is mad, and the King and Laertes plan a duel with Hamlet in which Laertes will use a poisoned foil.

Hamlet is wounded, switches swords and kills Laertes, who confesses to him before he dies. His mother drinks from a poisoned cup meant for him, and he stabs Claudius and forces him to drink poison. Then he, too, dies.

Such is the melodramatic outline of the greatest of all rôles. Arguments rage around every aspect of Hamlet, but especially over his fatal delay. The part can be played an infinite number of ways, so rich and complex is the character, and every age has its share of Hamlets of 'our times', political, religious, poetic. However he is played, he remains the ultimate Shakespeare man, a supreme creation matchless in verse, soliloquy, thought and humanity. He is the ideal Renaissance Man who has a 'noble mind' and is 'the expectancy and rose of the fair state', as Ophelia says when she thinks he is mad. Is he too sensitive to seek revenge? Is he paralysed by melancholy? Is he incapable of accepting the consequences of his destiny? Lack of space forbids more discussion. Millions of words about him exist, none of which ultimately explain the power of Hamlet in the theatre and in the minds of generation after generation. *Hamlet*

HARCOURT: An officer who tells Henry that Northumberland and Lord Bardolph have been defeated. *2 Henry IV*

HASTINGS, LORD: A rebel leader who decides to accept Prince John's offer of peace, but when his men have been dismissed, he is arrested and executed. *2 Henry IV*

He supports Edward IV and helps him escape after being captured by Warwick. *3 Henry VI*. He refuses to support Richard's attempt to seize the throne. In a grim scene, Richard turns on him, accuses him of being a traitor and of consorting with 'that harlot strumpet (Jane) Shore', and orders him beheaded. 'O bloody Richard! miserable England!' he laments, blaming himself for not acting against Richard. His head is brought to the gloating tyrant, to whom he later appears as a ghost before Bosworth, after which he appears to Richmond. *Richard III*

HECATE: This goddess of the moon, the earth and the underworld twice appears to the Witches to scold them for having acted without first consulting her. *Macbeth*

HECTOR: Priam's eldest son, and husband of Andromache. In a cynical play, he is the one famous character to emerge with his fame almost untarnished. But even he does not remain unscathed. He argues with Paris and Troilus that Helen should be given back to the Greeks, but, after sound reasoning about peace and morality, is swayed by thoughts of honour and renown, then admits he has challenged 'the dull and factious nobles of the Greeks' to single combat. Soon he is 'i' the vein of chivalry'. He fights inconclusively with Ajax, then, against the pleas of his family, goes off to fight his last battle, being 'engaged to many Greeks' to meet them. 'There is a thousand Hectors in the field' reports Nestor. Hector finally takes off his armour and rests, only to be murdered by Achilles and his followers. *Troilus and Cressida*

HELEN: An attendant of Imogen's. *Cymbeline*

The wife of Menelaus whose abduction by Paris has led to the Trojan War. Her part is small, and she is presented as being almost as vacuous as a 'dumb blonde', in keeping with the cynical tone of the play. *Troilus and Cressida*

HELENA: The play's controversial heroine. The orphaned daughter of a great physician, she has become the ward of the Countess Rousillon and loves her son Bertram, a boorish youth who has no interest in her. When he goes to Court at Paris, she follows to see him and try and cure the King of a fatal illness with a remedy of her father's. She says her life will be forfeit if she fails, but if she succeeds her reward must be the husband of her choice. She cures the King and picks the appalled Bertram, who, apart from not loving her, considers her beneath him. The King orders him to marry her.
He leaves her for Florence and the wars, saying he will only act as a husband if she can get a ring off his finger and a child by him. She manages this by taking the place in bed of Diana of Florence, whom Bertram wants to seduce, and in the end achieves her ends. Shakespeare's 'loveliest character' sighed Coleridge, but others have dubbed her a calculating little opportunist and even a revolting character. *All's Well that Ends Well*

An Athenian girl who loves Demetrius, but he, like Lysander, loves Hermia. Unfortunately, in the wood, where she goes to find Demetrius, Puck, trying to set things right, causes both men to be in love with her. He finally sets matters straight, however, and, in the end, Helena gets her Demetrius, but not before there have been some splendid misunderstandings and rows. In one we learn that Helena is tall, Hermia short—'You puppet you!' Helena describes her rival. *A Midsummer Night's Dream*

HELENUS: A priest and one of Priam's sons. In the argument between Hector, Troilus, Priam, Paris and himself about whether to give Helen back, he accuses Troilus of not giving reasons for keeping her. *Troilus and Cressida*

HELICANUS: A lord of Tyre, whom Pericles leaves to govern for him while he goes to Tarsus. Pericles is away so long that Helicanus is urged to take over the sovereignty, but he refuses, saying that Pericles should be sought for. A man of 'truth, of faith, of loyalty', says Gower in the Epilogue. *Pericles*

HENRY IV: He first appears as Henry Bolingbroke, son of John of Gaunt, and the tough usurper of his cousin's throne. At the start he accuses Mowbray of killing Gloucester, the King's uncle. Richard orders a trial by combat, but suddenly banishes Mowbray for life and Bolingbroke for ten years. He returns with an army after Richard confiscates the property left him by his father. Carrying all before him, he executes two of Richard's favourites, Bushy and Green, then captures the King, still protesting that he has only come to get his estates back. However, he deposes Richard, who is later murdered. The new King admits he had wanted Richard dead but spurns Exton who has killed him. He says he will go to the Holy Land as a penance. *Richard II*

At his next appearance, he has aged and is suspicious and 'wan with care', comparing his wastrel son to Hotspur, who is soon leading a rebellion against him. He criticizes his son, who promises to redeem himself and outstrip Hotspur. Father and son defeat the rebels at Shrewsbury. *1 Henry IV*

Henry's conscience over deposing Richard is causing him sleepless nights, made worse by the duties of kingship. Even the crushing of another rebellion cannot cheer him. He takes to his bed and wakens to find that Prince Hal has taken the crown from his bedside, thinking him dead. The two are reconciled. He realizes that he has become ill in the Jerusalem Chamber in Westminster and, recalling a prophecy that he would die in Jerusalem, asks to be taken back to the Chamber to die. *2 Henry IV*

HENRY V: He first appears as the 'madcap' Hal, Prince of Wales, bosom friend of Falstaff. After telling the fat knight he will not help rob travellers at Gadshill, his friend Poins persuades him to pretend to join and then rob the robbers. Back at the Boar's Head Tavern, Falstaff boasts of his bravery until punctured by Hal, but says he knew it was him all along. The King sends for him and before he goes, he and Falstaff play a mock scene about the royal meeting with Hal playing Henry. The King himself compares his son unfavourably with Hotspur, the rebel leader, and Hal promises to outstrip him, which he does at Shrewsbury, where he kills Hotspur. His eventual rejection of Falstaff has been lined up in the first scene—'I know you all, and will uphold The unyoked humour of your idleness', which repels today's audiences but not probably Elizabethans who had to be sure that their admired Henry V would reform. *1 Henry IV*

Hal and Poins pretend to be drawers to see the real Falstaff, who is disparaging about Hal to his mistress, Doll Tearsheet. Both are called to the wars. Later, Hal thinks his father is dead, takes his crown and the hurt father upbraids him. The two are finally reconciled. Hal becomes King, tells his brothers and even his enemy, the Lord Chief Justice, who once arrested him, that they have nothing to fear: his youthful follies are past. After his Coronation he publicly rejects Falstaff to the horror of all today's Falstaffians, but not, perhaps, his Elizabethan admirers, who understood better that it had to be. *2 Henry IV*

He becomes an idealized hero more than (by Shake-spearean standards) a whole man. With the Church's blessing he claims the French throne, rejects an insulting present of tennis balls from the Dauphin, and sets out for France, pausing at Southampton to have Cambridge, Scroop and Grey executed for treason. He takes Harfleur ('Once more into the breach, dear friends'), and marches towards Calais, telling the French herald that he will fight despite lack of numbers. The night before Agincourt, he gives his men 'a little touch of Harry in the night', wandering through the camp unknown. He talks seriously about war and duty with some of them, and reflects on kingship. After the Crispin's Day speech he defeats the French and returns in triumph to England. He goes back to France to make peace, and woos the French King's daughter, Katharine, bluntly, but pleasantly, and becomes heir to the French throne.

As the Chorus says, 'most greatly liv'd This star of England', and though some modern tastes find him chauvinistic and too patriotic, millions down the years have followed Elizabethan admirers in enjoying his story. *Henry V*

HENRY VI: The mild, weak, religious King. He appears as a youth after the fatal plucking of white and red roses to warn Gloucester and Winchester how civil war is a 'viperous worm That gnaws the bowels of the Commonwealth'. He creates Richard Plantaganet, Duke of York, then goes to France to be crowned. He orders Talbot to chastise Burgundy who has gone over to his fellow-countrymen, and tries to stop his nobles quarrelling: though he wears a red rose he loves both sides. To promote peace he agrees to marry a relative of the French King, then is persuaded by Suffolk to marry Margaret of Anjou. *1 Henry VI*

The marriage causes complications and Gloucester and York are both after his crown. He has to banish Gloucester's wife and strip Gloucester from his office as Protector. He faints when he learns of Gloucester's death and later learns he has been murdered. He and his tough wife, who despises him, fight the Yorkists at St. Albans and are forced to flee. *2 Henry VI*

To the disgust of his followers, he makes York his heir in place of his own son. The Wars of the Roses erupt again. At Towton, Margaret and Clifford send him from the battle and in a moving speech he wishes he could be a shepherd and that his death might bring peace. He watches a son that has killed his father in the fight and a father that has killed his son. Forced to flee to Scotland, he returns home only to be captured and to learn that Edward IV is now king. Warwick restores him to the throne, but Edward captures him, and he is murdered by Gloucester in the Tower, forgiving his murderer as he dies. *3 Henry VI*

HENRY VII: *see* Richmond

HENRY VIII: The rather characterless hero, patriotic, but led astray by Wolsey, and drawn so as not to offend by Shakespeare and, probably, Fletcher.
The King is first seen waiting to hear Buckingham's defence against a charge of high treason. He agrees to lessen certain taxes at Queen Katharine's request. He meets Anne Bullen and, egged on by Wolsey, asks Cardinal Campeius to come from Rome to judge the validity of his 20-year-old marriage, because he married his dead brother's wife. At the trial of Queen Katharine, Henry praises her and publicly hopes his marriage will be declared lawful. Then he decides to marry the Protestant Anne though Wolsey wants him to marry a French duchess. He finds Wolsey has been plotting behind his back with the Pope and that he has made a huge fortune. Henry causes his downfall, then marries Anne and has her crowned Queen. He protects his new Archbishop of Canterbury, Cranmer, from the attacks of Gardiner and others, who claim he is a heretic, and has him christen the infant Elizabeth, telling Cranmer how happy his prophecies about her have made him. *Henry VIII*

HENRY, PRINCE: The King's son who appears in the last scene with his dying father, and becomes Henry III. *King John*

HERALD: An English herald appears after Agincourt to give the King lists of English and French casualties. *Henry V*

A herald appears near the end of the play summoning any man maintaining that Edmund is a 'manifold traitor' to appear at the third sound of a trumpet. *King Lear*

HERBERT, SIR WALTER: One of Richmond's supporters at Bosworth. *Richard III*

HERMIA: The daughter of Egeus, who insists that she marry Demetrius, while she loves Lysander. They run away to the wood where Puck's magic accidentally makes both Demetrius and Lysander love Helena. Puck later gets his magic right and Hermia and Lysander are united, but there have been many misunderstandings in the meantime, in one of which—a blazing row between the two girls—we learn that Hermia is the shorter of the two. 'You puppet you!' shouts Helena, and Hermia calls her a painted maypole in return. *A Midsummer Night's Dream*

HERMIONE: The wife of Leontes, King of Sicilia, who falsely accuses her of adultery with Polixenes. Having first met her as a charming, witty woman, we now see her nobility, dignity and strength. Imprisoned, she gives birth to a daughter that Leontes calls 'a bastard by Polixenes'. He sends the child away to be exposed and die, but she survives, reappearing later as Perdita.

Meanwhile, the Queen is tried, not only for adultery but for conspiring to murder him. Even a message from the Oracle fails to convince Leontes. News is brought that their small son, Mamillius, has died from fear for his mother, who swoons. Leontes at last comes to his senses, but the Queen is reported to be dead too. Sixteen years later a penitent Leontes is shown a statue of Hermione, which turns out to be Hermione herself. She has lived in seclusion down the years waiting for her vindication. *The Winter's Tale*

HERO: Leonato's daughter. Claudio falls in love with her and they are soon betrothed. She, meanwhile, enters a conspiracy to get her beloved cousin, Beatrice, married to Benedick. But she is involved in a real conspiracy. Don John, determined to stop her marriage, arranges that Claudio and Don Pedro shall see one of his men, Borachio, apparently making love to her at a window.

Hero goes to church to be married, only to find herself

savagely denounced by Claudio as a wanton. She faints and Friar Francis, who believes her innocent, says she is dead, hoping to establish her innocence. The plot is revealed and a repentant Claudio is all set to marry Leonato's niece to make amends when he finds that the niece is Hero. She proceeds to help her cousin's marriage prospects by producing a poem written by Beatrice showing her love for Benedick. A modest figure beside her witty cousin, but an appealing one. *Much Ado About Nothing*

HIPPOLYTA: The Queen of the Amazons, betrothed to Theseus. She comforts him by telling him that the four days to their wedding will quickly pass. In the final scene she, like the rest of the aristocratic audience, mocks the troupe performing 'Pyramus and Thisbe'. *A Midsummer Night's Dream*

HOLOFERNES: A very pedantic schoolmaster. He flaunts his classical knowledge and grammatical skill at Sir Nathaniel and Dull and later suggests that 'The Nine Worthies' be performed before the Princess, with himself as Judas Maccabaeus. However, he only manages a few lines before being forced to retire by his audience's taunts. *Love's Labour's Lost*

HORATIO: The Prince's close friend and a moderate and restrained contrast to Hamlet. He sees the Ghost before Hamlet does, informs him about the apparition and accompanies him to the battlements to see it. Hamlet tells him how much he values him just before the Play Scene and warns him to watch Claudius's reaction to the play. While Hamlet is away, Horatio is asked to comfort the mad Ophelia. He joins Hamlet on his return and is with him at the end holding him in his arms as he is dying. Horatio tries to kill himself, but Hamlet urges him to live and tell his story. His epitaph over his friend is famous—'Goodnight, sweet Prince, And flights of angels sing thee to thy rest!' When Fortinbras arrives he tells him that he will give a full account of the tragedy. *Hamlet*

HORNER: An armourer who is accused by his apprentice, Peter Thump, of saying that Richard of York is the rightful heir to the throne. He denies the charge and accuses Thump of spite. Gloucester orders a trial by combat fought with sandbags in front of the King. Peter kills the drunken Horner who confesses just before he dies. *2 Henry VI*

HORTENSIO: A young man who tempts his friend Petruchio to woo Katharina by telling him about her vast dowry. Hortensio does this so that he himself can try and win her sister, Bianca. He manages to get to see her by disguising himself as a music teacher, but finally loses her to Lucentio. He promptly consoles himself with a widow. *The Taming of the Shrew*

HORTENSIUS: A servant of one of Timon's creditors, who fails to get payment. *Timon of Athens*

HOST: An old man who takes Julia to the Duke's Palace. They see Proteus serenading Silvia, and the Host tells her that Proteus lodges with him. *The Two Gentlemen of Verona*

The cheerful, practical-joking landlord of the Garter Inn. When Caius and Evans plan to fight a duel he fools them by telling each a different rendezvous, but when he confesses to them, they rob him of three horses. Fenton offers him £100 to help him elope, which cheers him up, and he finds a priest for the wedding. *The Merry Wives of Windsor*

HOSTESS: She appears in the Induction, where she goes to fetch a constable to arrest the drunken Sly, who is refusing to pay for glasses he has broken. *The Taming of the Shrew*

HOTSPUR: The nickname of Henry Percy, a minor character. *Richard II*. A marvel of a secondary rôle. *1 Henry IV*. With his father, Northumberland, he joins Bolingbroke and helps him become Henry IV. *Richard II*. He later leads a rebellion against Henry. *1 Henry IV*
The quarrel has started after the King has demanded that Hotspur should hand over prisoners won at Homildon.

Hotspur volcanically defends his actions to the King and refuses to hand over his prisoners unless Henry ransoms Mortimer, Hotspur's brother-in-law, who has just married his captor, Glendower's, daughter. When the King angrily leaves, Hotspur explodes again, railing at him as a usurper. His uncle, Worcester, suggests the rebellion.

We next meet him at Warkworth, his home, his mind on the forthcoming rebellion but having time to tease his wife affectionately. In Wales, he quarrels with Mortimer and Glendower over dividing the kingdom and teases the latter for his belief in portents. He is the very heart of the rebellion before the Battle of Shrewsbury, undaunted by his father's and Glendower's absence. Worcester fails to tell him the King's generous terms and he is killed in the battle by Hal, Falstaff taking the credit and carrying the body from the field. For dramatic reasons Shakespeare makes Hotspur and Hal the same age: the real Hotspur was twenty-three years older.

'Gunpowder Percy' is at once a living volcano, valiant, witty and reckless, the focus of English chivalry, and, in the scenes with his wife, human and boisterously tender. A theme of the play is Honour. To Falstaff it is a mere word: he wants none of Hotspur's Honour, a tangible thing that can be plucked from 'the pale-faced moon'. Falstaff's attitude to war must have seemed common sense to a belligerent Elizabethan audience, yet Shakespeare's divine neutrality makes Hotspur's ultra-romantic attitude seem right too. *1 Henry IV*

Hotspur is one of several characters—others include Falstaff, Hamlet, Mercutio and the Bastard—with whom Shakespeare seems to identify himself so completely and vividly that they remain unique in drama. His habit of speaking 'thick', referred to by Lady Percy, is usually played as a stammer.

HUBERT DE BURGH: King John hands over his nephew, Prince Arthur, to his Chamberlain, Hubert, and orders him to kill the boy. John's written orders state that he is to be blinded, which Hubert cannot bring himself to do. He hides the boy and tells John he is dead. Arthur later dies trying to escape and the nobles' suspicions fall on Hubert, who is saved by the intervention of the Bastard. Hubert has a classic concise exchange with John: King: 'Death.' Hubert: 'My Lord?' King: 'A grave.' Hubert: 'He shall not live.' *King John*

HUME: A priest hired by Cardinal Beaufort and Suffolk to help the Duchess of Gloucester, eager for her husband to be king, find out the future of sorcery. He procures the witch, Margery Jourdain, and a conjurer named Bolingbroke to provide the black magic, but they are caught in the act by Buckingham and York. Hume is sentenced to hang. *2 Henry VI*

HUNTSMEN: The Lord's companions in the Induction. *The Taming of the Shrew*

HYMEN: The God of Marriage appears to restore Rosalind to her father and perform the marriage ritual. *As You Like It*

I

IACHIMO: An Italian whom the banished Posthumus meets in Rome. He wagers that he can seduce Posthumus's wife, Imogen, who is still in Britain. Though he fails, he manages to get into her room by hiding in a trunk. He gets out when she is asleep, steals her bracelet and tells Posthumus that he has succeeded, adding enough detail to make him believe the story. Later he joins the army that invades Britain, and, after being captured, confesses his crime and is pardoned by Posthumus. *Cymbeline*

IAGO: The villain whose 'motiveless malignity' (Coleridge) hidden beneath an 'honest' exterior, causes Othello the Moor's downfall.

Iago is Othello's ensign and hates him for promoting Michael Cassio as his Lieutenant instead of himself. Othello has secretly married Desdemona, and Iago arouses her father, Brabantio, to tell him about it. After Othello has explained himself to the Senate, Iago is appointed to escort Desdemona to Cyprus. He broods over Othello's alleged seduction of his wife, Emilia, and decides to tell the gullible Othello that Desdemona and Cassio are lovers.

In Cyprus, he engineers Cassio's disgrace by making him aggressively drunk, then suggests that Cassio ask Desdemona to plead his case to Othello. He sets to work to arouse the 'green-eyed monster' jealousy in Othello, finally achieving his aim by seeing that Cassio finds, and is seen holding, a handkerchief that Othello has given to Desdemona.

Meanwhile, he has reduced Othello to an epileptic fit, and sees to it that he watches Iago and Cassio laughingly talk about Cassio's mistress when Othello thinks they are discussing Desdemona.

Iago arranges for his foolish crony, Roderigo, to kill Cassio, but he fails, and Iago kills him to silence him. After Othello has killed his wife, Iago's villainy is revealed. He kills Emilia, but Othello fails to kill him. We leave the 'hellish villain' awaiting torture.

Some see Iago as pure evil, others the personification of the Medieval morality character, Vice, still others as a monstrous practical-joker. The part is a magnificent one, only weakened if Iago appears too villainous and makes Othello seem over foolish. *Othello*

IDEN, ALEXANDER: A Kentish gentleman in whose garden the defeated rebel, Cade, hides. Iden does not want to fight a starving man, but is forced to. When he kills him and finds it is Cade, he takes his head to Henry and is knighted. *2 Henry VI*

IMOGEN: Cymbeline's attractive and brave daughter. She has fallen from favour by marrying Posthumus Leonatus, a 'poor but worthy gentleman', who is banished. In Italy, he meets Iachimo who wagers he can seduce Imogen. She spurns him, but he gets into her bedroom in a trunk and, while she is asleep, steals her bracelet and notes a mole on her breast. His circumstantial evidence convinces Posthumus that his wife is unfaithful and he orders his servant, Pisanio, to kill her.

Meanwhile, Imogen has spurned the evil Queen's lumpish son, Cloten, her stepbrother, telling him she prefers Posthumus's meanest garment to him. She sets out to Milford Haven with Pisanio, thinking she is going to meet Posthumus, but the servant tells her he is meant to kill her. She disguises herself as a boy, Fidele, and agrees to try and enter the service of the Roman general, Lucius, and get to Rome to confront her husband. After wandering through Wales she comes upon the cave of Belarius, unjustly banished by her father, from whom he stole two infants and brought them up as his sons. They are Imogen's brothers. They like Fidele and lament her apparent death from a drug. Cloten, who has pursued her, is killed by one of her brothers, and when she wakes, she thinks his headless body is her husband's. She joins Lucius, and, after he has been defeated by the British, meets her father again, exposes Iachimo and is reunited with a repentant Posthumus. *Cymbeline*

IRAS: A loyal attendant of Cleopatra's who appears in a number of scenes. When Cleopatra imagines a 'squeaking' boy playing her on a stage boying her greatness 'i' the posture of a whore', Iras tells her she would rather scratch her own eyes out with her nails than watch. She dresses the Queen in her robe and crown, then dies after being kissed by her. *Antony and Cleopatra*

IRIS: A spirit who plays Juno's messenger in the Masque. She personifies her 'watery arch'—the rainbow. *The Tempest*

ISABEL: The French Queen who gives her blessing to her daughter Katharine's marriage to Henry. *Henry V*

ISABELLA: The play's controversial heroine. She is a novice in a convent, and when her brother, Claudio, is imprisoned by Angelo for immorality, Claudio's friend, Lucio, brings her a message asking her to intercede with Angelo. He agrees to release him if she will give herself to him. Despite her brother's pleas, she refuses, calling him a coward. The disguised Duke of Vienna suggests that she shall pretend to give into Angelo, but her place in Angelo's bed shall be taken by Mariana, who he has deserted though he was once betrothed to her. Angelo still orders Claudio's execution, but the order is disobeyed. The Duke reappears as himself, pretends not to believe Isabella and Mariana, but then makes Angelo marry Mariana, Claudio the girl he has seduced and announces that he will try to marry Isabella himself.

Saint or icicle? Martyr or pitiless prig? 'Better it were a brother died at once, Than that a sister, by redeeming him, Should die for ever,' she says, and she also has very fine speeches pleading for mercy. *Measure for Measure*

J

JAMY, CAPTAIN: A Scottish captain at Harfleur, and a valiant soldier and an expert in military history, according to the Welshman, Fluellen. The two converse with the Irishman, Macmorris. *Henry V*

JAQUENETTA: A country wench who is loved by both Costard and Don Armado. The Don has Costard imprisoned for consorting with her, and later the two almost fight over her. *Love's Labour's Lost*

JAQUES: A melancholy lord of the banished Duke's. His famous and cynical review of the Seven Ages of Man, beginning 'All the world's a stage', is the best known speech in the play, from whose action he stands detached. However, he makes Touchstone marry Audrey, and weeps over a wounded deer. Travel, and presumably, what he has done on his travels, has made him sad, and at the end he goes out to begin a religious life with the reformed Duke Frederick. *As You Like It*

JAQUES DE BOYS: This brother of Orlando and Oliver appears at the end bringing the news that Duke Frederick, on his way to kill his exiled brother, has met a hermit, who has converted him. *As You Like It*

JESSICA: Shylock's lively daughter. Hating her home and ashamed to be her father's daughter, she disguises herself as a boy and elopes with Lorenzo, taking a casket of Shylock's jewels. At Belmont, Portia's house, she and Lorenzo have a love scene famous for its beautiful verse. *The Merchant of Venice*

JEWELLER: He calls on Timon as his generous patron. *Timon of Athens*

JOAN LA PUCELLE (JOAN OF ARC): A witch and a whore, Shakespeare getting his 'facts' from Holinshed. As a 'holy maid' she meets the Dauphin, spurns his advances, gains his respect and raises the siege of Orleans. She captures Rouen and then persuades the Duke of Burgundy to desert the English for the French. After conjuring up fiends and offering her 'body, soul and all' for a French victory, she is captured by York and tried. She claims to be descended from kings and to be a pure virgin; but when she is condemned to be burnt, announces she is pregnant by Alençon, and is borne off cursing, with York calling her a 'foul minister of hell'. *1 Henry VI*

JOHN, DON: Don Pedro's villainous bastard brother. Defeated after fighting against his brother, he is determined to be revenged on his victor, young Claudio. He falls in with a plan devised by a henchman to slander Claudio's betrothed, Hero, by making her seem unfaithful.

After his success, he flees, but we later learn that he has been captured and is being brought back to suffer 'brave punishments' of Benedick's devising. *Much Ado About Nothing*

JOHN, KING: The name part, if not exactly the hero, of the play. He defends his country against foreign—and Catholic—powers. However, his machinations to have Prince Arthur, the rightful heir, killed loses our sympathy. But the rôle, part villain, part patriot, part hysteric, is a fine one. At the start, John is told by the French ambassador to give up his throne to Arthur. He angrily says he will invade France, which he proceeds to do. Peace comes about when his niece Blanch marries the Dauphin. At the wedding festivities, the Pope's legate attacks John for not allowing the new archbishop, Langton, to take his See. John rejects his demands and is excommunicated, the French King being forced to break the peace. John wins the ensuing battle, captures Arthur and orders Hubert to kill him. Though this does not take place, Arthur dies trying to escape, and many of John's nobles desert him for the Dauphin who is invading England. John yields to the Pope and the Papal Legate says he will ensure that the French cease fighting. The Dauphin has other ideas, but his enemy, John, is taken ill in battle, then poisoned by a monk.

Perhaps his finest scene is where he assails Hubert for killing Arthur, though he has given him orders to do just that. His death scene, too, is a fine one, as the guilty, treacherous monarch feverishly laments: 'Within me there is a hell.' *King John*

JOHN OF GAUNT: Richard II's uncle and the father of Bolingbroke, later Henry IV. The most illustrious figure in the kingdom, he has to endure the banishment of his son, which helps bring him to his deathbed. The dying man speaks the famous patriotic speech, beginning 'This royal throne of kings', then, when the King visits him, warns him against flatterers and misusing funds. Richard calls him 'a lunatic, lean-witted fool' and tells him that if he were not who he is, he would be beheaded. He is carried off to die and his lands are confiscated, which provokes Bolingbroke's rebellion. *Richard II*

JOHN OF LANCASTER: *see* Bedford

JOURDAIN, MARGERY: A witch who helps conjure up a spirit to reveal the future to the Duchess of Gloucester who wants to be Queen. She is caught and condemned to be burnt at Smithfield. *2 Henry VI*

JULIA: In love with Proteus. When his friend, Valentine, goes to Milan, he stays at home to be near her, but his father insists that he goes there too. There he falls for Valentine's Silvia. The faithful Julia follows him, disguised as a boy, but finds him singing to Silvia. She becomes his servant, 'Sebastian' and has to carry the ring she gave him to Silvia. All ends surprisingly well when she reveals herself to Proteus. *The Two Gentlemen of Verona*

JULIET: She is betrothed to Claudio, and pregnant by him, which, by a new law, condemns him to death. She confesses to the disguised Duke that her sin is the heavier, and at the play's end, he orders Claudio to restore her honour by marrying her. *Measure for Measure*

The play's fourteen-year-old heroine, innocent, loving, sensual, witty, full of vitality and brave. She has much magnificent verse, which reaches great heights in her death scene.
She is a Capulet, her lover, Romeo, is a Montague and their families are feuding. Destined to marry Paris, she meets Romeo at a ball and they fall in love. After a very famous love scene, they are married secretly by Friar Laurence. But Romeo, to revenge his friend, Mercutio, is forced to kill Juliet's cousin, Tybalt, and is banished.
Juliet sends her Nurse to bring him to her for a last farewell and they spend the night together before he leaves for Mantua. Her father tells her she must marry Paris and the

Friar gives her a potion to make her seem dead. She will then be buried in the family tomb and be rescued by Romeo. But his plans go awry. Juliet wakes to find that Romeo, finding her apparently dead, has killed himself, so she stabs herself and dies.

This brief account leaves out Juliet's isolation, which builds as her family, even her beloved Nurse, pressurize her into agreeing to marry Paris. Her position is truly pitiful and tragic and the part is a great one. *Romeo and Juliet*

K

KATHARINA: The daughter of Baptista of Padua who insists that she marry before her younger sister Bianca, who has plenty of suitors. Katharina, being fiery and outspoken to the point of shrewishness, has none, though Baptista has settled a large dowry on her.

Petruchio, an adventurer, decides to woo her, not only to help his friend Hortensio gain Bianca, but because he wants the Shrew's dowry. She abuses and assaults him while he woos her, but he wins her, and carries her off to his country house, where she is starved and ill-treated into submission, after which the utterly tamed and subdued girl is taken back to Padua. To everyone's surprise, Katharina is now so submissive that Petruchio wins a bet from two other husbands that he has the most submissive wife.

Shakespeare plays fair with his Shrew. Though she is violent, much of it is clearly due to jealousy of her sister who is as admired by men as much as she is avoided. She also is only too well aware that Baptista much prefers Bianca. The play is mainly broad farce and horseplay, but that does not nullify the relationship and strong attraction between the principal sparring partners. *The Taming of the Shrew*

KATHARINE: One of the Princess of France's attendants. Dumain, one of the young men who have forsworn women, along with the King of Navarre, falls in love with her and she with him. At the play's end, when she leaves with the Princess of France, she promises that she will marry Dumain if he will wait until she returns with the Princess in a year, always assuming she still has 'much love' for him. *Love's Labour's Lost*

The daughter of the French King. We meet her first having an English lesson with her lady, Alice. Later, she is wooed by Henry who is determined to marry her as part of the peace treaty with France. She seems very pleased with the arrangement, even though she tells him French girls should not be kissed before marriage. She responds readily when he breaks the rules. *Henry V*

Katharine of Aragon, King Henry VIII's first wife. At first she is still in favour and able to get Henry to lessen taxes that Wolsey has imposed. Henry meets Anne Bullen and, egged on by Wolsey, thinks about divorcing Katharine because she was originally married to his dead brother, Arthur. The Queen is tried, but refuses to stay at the trial after reminding Henry that she has been a 'true and humble wife'. She says she will appeal to the Pope. Wolsey and Campeius fail to make her give up her title. Later, divorced, lonely and sick, she speaks charitably of her old enemy, Wolsey. She has a vision of six white figures bidding her farewell. Then she receives Capucius, the Emperor's emissary. She sends the King a message of forgiveness and pleads for her 'wretched women', then is led away to die.

Katharine, the 'most unhappy woman living' is a most moving and sympathetic part. Even Henry apparently still loves her in his way. No cipher, she defends herself with courage and queenly dignity. She is as noble as she is blameless. *Henry VIII*

KENT, EARL OF: A servant of the King whose blunt, manly defence of Cordelia when she is disinherited by Lear gets him banished. Determined still to serve his master, he disguises himself as a servant, Caius, and asks Lear to employ him—'you have that in your countenance which I would fain call master . . . Authority.' When Goneril's servant, Oswald, insults Lear, Kent trips him up; later he insults Oswald and beats him with a sword. Despite the fact that he is Lear's messenger, Cornwall puts him in the stocks. Lear and the Fool find him and he is later released. He is with Lear in the storm and takes him to Dover to join Cordelia. He is mortally wounded in the battle which follows but is reunited as himself with his dying master. Told by Albany to help rule the kingdom, he replies that he has a journey ahead of him—'My master calls me, I must not say no.' Utterly loyal, but perhaps too tactless and quick to anger, and therefore liable to make things worse for Lear, Kent is a gift part for a good actor. *King Lear*

L

LAERTES: The son of Polonius and brother of Ophelia. We first meet the hot-tempered young man advising her not to believe Hamlet's avowals of love, after which Polonius gives him some advice before he sets off to return to school in France. He erupts back to Elsinore to demand an explanation of his father's death of Claudius, and finds his sister is mad. Claudius suggests how Laertes can accidentally kill Hamlet with a poisoned foil and he agrees. The Queen arrives to describe Orphelia's death. He later leaps into her grave to embrace her body, then fights in the grave with Hamlet. In the ensuing duel Laertes wounds Hamlet, but, when the foils are switched, is himself fatally wounded. He asks Hamlet's forgiveness before he dies. *Hamlet*

LAFEU (LAFEW): An old lord who escorts Helena to Paris. He is furious because the courtiers are not keen to marry her and keeps quarrelling with Parolles who he detests, warning Bertram against him. But when Parolles is exposed as a coward, he treats him generously. When Helena is thought dead, he offers Bertram his own daughter for a wife and, when all ends well, he says 'Mine eyes smell onions.' *All's Well that Ends Well*

LANCASTER, PRINCE JOHN OF: *see* Bedford

LARTIUS, TITUS: A Roman general who helps Coriolanus defeat the Volscians at Corioli and he is left in command of the city by Cominius. He later tells Coriolanus that Aufidius has gone to Antium, also that the Volscian hates him more than anything on earth. *Coriolanus*

LAUNCE: A Clown, the servant of Proteus, and the owner of the splendidly sour-natured dog, Crab. Most of his scenes are with this ill-trained cur who is liable to make a whole room smell, or with Speed, the servant of Valentine. At one point he is ordered by Proteus to take a dog to Silvia, but loses it and offers Crab instead. *The Two Gentlemen of Verona*

LAURENCE, FRIAR: *see* Friar Laurence

LAVACHE: A clown in the Countess's Household. He gets sent away for justifying adultery. He later shows her how 'O Lord, sir' will serve as an answer to any question, and, being established as a well bred man, is sent to Helena at the French Court with a message. Carrying letters is his main function, apart from showing his verbal dexterity. *All's Well that Ends Well*

LAVINIA: Titus's daughter. The Emperor Saturninus, with the agreement of Titus, says he will marry her, but Bassianus, the Emperor's brother, carries her off and marries her. He is murdered by Demetrius and Chiron, sons of the evil Tamora, Queen of the Goths, who encourages them to rape Lavinia and see that she does not betray them. They cut off her hands and cut out her tongue.

She can find no way of telling her father who has attacked her until at last she manages to open a copy of Ovid's 'Metamorphoses' at the story of Philomel and how she was raped. She then traces out her attackers' names using a staff in her mouth. Titus kills the pair, Lavinia holding a basin for their blood in her stumps, then kills her to end her shame just before serving the rapists to their mother baked in a pie. *Titus Andronicus*

LAWYER: He plucks a white rose in the Temple Gardens, so becomes a Yorkist. *1 Henry VI*

LEAR: The play's tragic hero. He intends to abdicate by dividing Britain between his daughters Goneril, Regan and Cordelia, foolishly giving the biggest share of land to the one who says she loves him most. Unlike the hypocritical and soon to be proved monstrous Goneril and Regan, Cordelia cannot bring herself publicly to declare her love and Lear disinherits her.

He divides everything between the others and simply retains his title, saying that he and 100 men will live with Goneril and Regan in turn. He banishes Kent for speaking up for Cordelia, who marries the King of France, a worthy man, not deterred by her lack of a dowry.

Lear's first stay—with Goneril—ends in his damning her after she has complained about his unruly knights and allowed her steward Oswald to insult him. He arrives at Gloucester's castle to find his servant (actually Kent in disguise) in the stocks on the orders of Regan's husband, Cornwall. Regan now joins Goneril in upbraiding Lear and he leaves, swearing revenge on them. The gates are barred on him.

On a heath in a storm he starts to lose his reason. He shelters in a hovel with his Fool and is then taken to a farmhouse by Gloucester, who tells Kent to get Lear to Dover as his life is threatened. Lear reaches Dover quite mad. Dressed in flowers, he meets Gloucester, who has been blinded by Cornwall. The King is taken to the camp of Cordelia's husband who has invaded Britain to help him and wakes to a touching reunion with Cordelia. But she and her husband's army is defeated and Lear and she are taken prisoner. They are ordered to be hanged and Lear enters with Cordelia dead in his arms, then dies himself.

Lear is a titanic figure whose rages, impulsiveness and foolishness bring about his downfall and madness. He comes out of his ordeal sanely and grandly, with a nobility unseen in him at first, when he appeared a near-senile tyrant, except to those who knew him best like Kent who saw Authority in his face. Shakespeare charts his road to madness brilliantly. Seeing how the unfortunate live gives him insight which prepares us for the tragic, pitiful figure of later scenes. His overwhelming language, which he uses at times to call the very elements to help him, is as stupendous as his quieter moments, such as when he wakes to find Cordelia by him, are deeply moving. He dies thinking she still lives. Few actors have scaled this Everest of a part to universal acclaim. *King Lear*

LE BEAU: A rather exotic courtier of Duke Frederick. He tells Rosalind and Celia about the prowess of Charles the wrestler and, after Orlando has defeated the champion, advises him to leave for his own safety. *As You Like It*

LENA, POPILIUS: A senator who, just before the assassination, wishes Brutus and Cassius that 'their enterprise today may thrive'. They see him talking to Caesar and fear he may be betraying their secret, but decide he is not. *Julius Caesar*

LENNOX: A Scottish noble, who goes to Duncan's room with Macbeth after the King's murder and sees Macbeth killing the allegedly guilty grooms. When he sees Macbeth's behaviour at the banquet at which the Ghost of Banquo appears, he decides that the new King is the murderer and flies to join Malcolm's rebel forces. *Macbeth*

LEONARDO: A servant of Bassanio. He is sent to buy a new livery for Launcelot Gobbo. *The Merchant of Venice*

LEONATO: The governor of Messina and father of Hero. A pleasant man, he is delighted when his daughter is betrothed to Claudio, even if he had half-hoped that Duke Pedro might have wed her. He is also anxious for his niece and ward, Beatrice, to be married, and cheerfully joins in the Don's conspiracy to match her with Benedick, even though he thinks the pair, once married, would 'talk themselves mad' in a week. When Hero is wrongly accused by Claudio before their wedding of betraying him, Leonato is so shaken by her apparent guilt that he wishes he had no daughter, but he agrees with a friar who believes her innocent, to pretend that she is dead. When Hero's innocence is proved, Claudio tells Leonato to impose a penance on him for his sin in doubting her. Leonato, not revealing that his daughter is still alive, tells him to marry his niece, whom, he says, is the copy of Hero. The niece is Hero. *Much Ado About Nothing*

LEONINE: A servant of Dionyza, who orders him to kill Marina because she overshadows her own daughter. He is about to murder her when pirates appear and he runs away, telling his mistress that Marina is dead. As a safety precaution, she poisons him. *Pericles*

LEONTES: King of Sicilia. He encourages his wife, Hermione, to persuade Polixenes, King of Bohemia, to stay longer with them, then wrongly suspects that they are lovers and that Polixenes is the father of the child she is expecting. He suspects that his son, Mamillius, is not his own and wants Polixenes poisoned, but Camillo, the lord asked to kill him, warns him and they flee.

Leontes then has Hermione arrested and her son removed from her. She has a daughter and he orders Antigonus to abandon the child on some deserted spot. He tries Hermione, but even when the Delphic oracle proclaims her innocent, will not believe it. Mamillius dies and Hermione faints at the news. Leontes comes to his senses, but the Queen is reported dead.

Sixteen years later, penitent and desperate, he promises

Paulina that he will not remarry except to a twin of Hermione. His unknown daughter, Perdita, arrives with her lover, Florizel, and Leontes is reunited with her. Paulina shows him a statue of Hermione which turns out to be—Hermione.

Leontes' devastating, ill-founded jealousy, which warps his mind to the point of diseased frenzy, suggests previous unbalance and weakness of character. *The Winter's Tale*

LEPIDUS, MARCUS AEMILIUS: He sees Caesar murdered and, though seemingly undistinguished, becomes one of the Triumvirate with Antony and Octavius. *Julius Caesar*. He tries to keep his colleagues on good terms. At the banquet on Pompey's galley he gets very drunk and is carried out. We learn later than he has been imprisoned by Octavius. *Antony and Cleopatra*

LEWIS XI: The French King who agrees to help Queen Margaret fight Edward IV. He later tells Warwick that his sister-in-law, Lady Bona, may marry Edward. *3 Henry VI*

LEWIS THE DAUPHIN: The son of Charles VI of France. He sends Henry tennis balls as an insult, and before Agincourt is in a boastful mood, saying his way 'shall be paved with English faces'. But in defeat he suggests stabbing himself. *Henry V*

Philip II of France's son. He marries Blanch, John's niece, which settles the quarrel between England and France. But when John is excommunicated war breaks out and the Dauphin is persuaded by the Papal legate to invade England and claim the throne. *King John*

LIEUTENANT OF THE TOWER: Henry's keeper, who when the King is released begs his pardon for what he has had to do. Henry thanks him for his kindness. He is again his keeper when Gloucester murders him. *3 Henry VI*

LIEUTENANT TO AUFIDIUS: He tells Aufidius that Coriolanus's triumphs have eclipsed his own. *Coriolanus*

LIGARIUS, CAIUS: One of the conspirators but not present at the assassination. He calls Brutus the 'soul of Rome'. *Julius Caesar*

LINCOLN, BISHOP OF: The King's confessor. As Henry reminds him at the trial of Katharine, he was the first to suggest that she should be divorced. *Henry VIII*

LODOVICO: A kinsman of Brabantio, Desdemona's father. He appears in Cyprus with a letter recalling Othello, who he sees striking his wife—'this would not be believ'd in Venice'. Emilia says he is a very handsome man. He helps Cassio when he is attacked by Roderigo, and appears at the end to promise the 'hellish villain' Iago slow torture. *Othello*

LONGAVILLE: One of the King of Navarre's three lords who have forsworn the company of women for a time. He falls in love with Maria, one of the Princess of France's ladies, and addresses the sonnet, 'Did the heavenly rhetoric of thine eye' to her. When the ladies return to France she promises to return to him in a year. *Love's Labour's Lost*

LORD: The most important Lord in Shakespeare is in the Prologue to *The Shrew*. Finding the drunken Sly, he abducts him, pretending Sly is a nobleman who has been mad for fifteen years. He orders his page to dress up as Sly's wife and has a comedy performed to cheer him up and cure him. The play proper follows. *The Taming of the Shrew*

LORD CHANCELLOR: Sir Thomas More is named to succeed Wolsey but does not appear. A nameless Chancellor (Sir Thomas Audley) appears in the Coronation procession, later another nameless Chancellor (Sir Thomas Wriothesley) is president of the Council which tries to imprison Cranmer for heresy until stopped by the King. *Henry VIII*

LORD CHIEF JUSTICE: He warns Falstaff about his evil ways and commands him to repay his debt to Mistress Quickly. He imprisons Prince Hal and later fears his revenge when the Prince becomes King. Henry keeps him in office and tells him to banish and imprison Falstaff. *2 Henry IV*

LORD MAYOR OF LONDON: The current Lord Mayor ends the fighting between the followers of Gloucester and Winchester in the city streets and asks the King to intervene in the quarrel. *1 Henry VI*

The Lord Mayor supports Richard's claim to the throne. *Richard III*

The Lord Mayor is at the young Elizabeth's christening. *Henry VIII*

LORENZO: A friend of Bassanio. He elopes with Jessica, Shylock's daughter, and goes to Belmont, Portia's home, which he is asked to manage while she is in Venice. He has a famous poetic love scene with Jessica: 'In such a night as this . . .' *The Merchant of Venice*

LOVEL, LORD: A henchman of Richard. He takes Hastings to be executed and laters returns with his head. *Richard III*

LOVELL, SIR THOMAS: The Chancellor of the Exchequer. At Buckingham's trial for high treason he hears Buckingham's treacherous surveyor say that he was to be beheaded. He later sneers at French fashions and, when leading Buckingham to the block, asks his forgiveness. He helps sway Henry against Wolsey, conspires with Gardiner in the abortive conspiracy against Cranmer, and tells Henry about Anne's illness after giving birth to Elizabeth. *Henry VIII*

LUCE: A servant of Adriana, who will not let Antipholus of Ephesus into his house as she thinks he is already there. *The Comedy of Errors*

LUCENTIO: Vincentio's student son and one of Bianca's suitors. He gets to see her by disguising himself as a tutor called Cambio, is successful and marries her secretly. He throws a banquet at the end of which Bianca proves less submissive a wife than her shrewish sister, Katharina. *The Taming of the Shrew*

LUCETTA: Julia's waiting woman who approves of Proteus as her suitor, comparing him favourably with his rivals. When Julia wants to join him in Milan, however, she at first tries to dissuade her. *The Two Gentlemen of Verona*

LUCIANA: Adriana's unmarried sister who mistakes Antipholus of Syracuse for her brother-in-law and is startled when he makes love to her. When the errors are resolved she appears all set to marry him. *The Comedy of Errors*

LUCIANUS: A character in the play performed before Claudius. He poisons the king for his estate. *Hamlet*

LUCILIUS: A supporter of Brutus and Cassius who tells Brutus that Cassius's friendship for him seems to be cooling. When he is captured at Philippi, he pretends to be Brutus. Antony admires his devotion and orders that he be well treated. *Julius Caesar*

One of Timon's servants. Timon gives him enough money to make him seem a suitable husband to the father of the girl he wants to marry. *Timon of Athens*

LUCIO: A 'fantastic' who asks Isabella to intercede with Angelo to spare her brother Claudio's life. He makes offensive comments about the Duke to a friar, not realizing that the friar is the Duke in disguise and later claims that the friar made the comments. The Duke forgives him, but makes him marry the woman he 'begot with child'. The immoral, talkative Lucio uselessly begs he shall not be forced to marry a whore. *Measure for Measure*

LUCIUS: A boy servant of Brutus. He admits the conspirators early in the play and on the day of Caesar's assassination is sent by Portia to see what is happening to her husband. Though he later twice falls asleep on duty, Brutus lets him rest. Before Philippi he promises to be good to Lucius 'if I do live'. *Julius Caesar*

One of Timon's false friends. He gives him four horses 'trapp'd in silver', but when Timon is ruined will not lend him money and even sends a servant to collect a debt. *Timon of Athens*

Titus's eldest son. Having endured the execution of his two brothers, his sister's rape and mutilation and his father's loss of a hand, he gains the aid of the Goths to help him fight the Emperor Saturninus. He kills him and becomes Emperor himself. He orders the wicked Tamora's body to be thrown to the beasts and has the villain, Aaron, set 'breast-deep in earth' and famished. *Titus Andronicus*

LUCIUS, YOUNG: Son of the above. His aunt, Lavinia, raped and mutilated, shows what has happened to her by managing to turn to the story of Philomel in his copy of Ovid's 'Metamorphoses'. He then takes a present of arrows and a threatening note from Titus to Demetrius and Chiron, Lavinia's assailants. *Titus Andronicus*

LUCIUS, CAIUS: *see* Caius Lucius

LUCIUS'S SERVANT: The servant of one of Timon's false friends who tries and fails to collect a debt from Timon. *Timon of Athens*

LUCULLUS: A false friend of Timon. He sends Timon two brace of greyhounds, but when Timon is ruined and his servant comes to ask Lucullus for a loan, the latter tries to bribe him to say he had not been able to find him. *Timon of Athens*

LUCY, SIR WILLIAM: An English leader who begs York and Somerset to help Talbot and later bitterly blames them for his defeat. He recovers the bodies of Talbot and his son. *1 Henry VI*

LYCHORIDA: Marina's nurse. In the storm at sea she brings the newly-born Marina to Pericles, but mistakenly tells him that his wife has died. She stays at Tarsus to look after Marina and is later reported dead. *Pericles*

LYMOGES: The Duke of Austria. Allied to Philip of France, he is first mocked by the Bastard, then killed by him near Angiers. *King John*

LYSANDER: An Athenian in love with Hermia, who is meant to marry Demetrius, her father, Egeus's, choice. Lysander and Hermia escape to the forest, where, owing to a mistake by Puck, he is magically made to love Helena instead. After much confusion and quarrelling, all is sorted out and Lysander and Hermia are reunited, with the Duke overruling the objections of Egeus. *A Midsummer Night's Dream*

LYSIMACHUS: Governor of Mytilene. On a visit to a brothel, he meets the virtuous Marina and is shamed by her goodness, giving her gold and promising her help. Wishing to marry her if he can be sure she is nobly born, he finds she is Pericles's long-lost daughter, and, after the two have been reunited, successfully claims her for a wife. *Pericles*

M

MACBETH: The tragic hero whose loyalty and nobility are eroded by ambition until he is reduced to despair and total moral collapse. As a general of King Duncan of Scotland he is returning from defeating rebels when witches tell him he will be Thane of Cawdor and King of Scotland 'hereafter'. The Thane is executed for treason and Duncan appoints Macbeth in his place.
His ambition is enflamed by the prophecy, and he returns to Glamis where his even more ambitious wife overrules his scruples and has him plan Duncan's murder when the King visits them. Macbeth stabs him, using servants' daggers to throw suspicion on them, but Lady Macbeth

has the courage to incriminate the grooms. The conscience-stricken Macbeth becomes King. He has his friend, Banquo, killed because of a prophecy by the witches that he would father kings, but Banquo's son escapes. His Ghost appears at a banquet and Macbeth reacts guiltily. He revisits the witches who comfort him with prophecies: that he will be safe until Birnam Wood comes to Dunsinane and that no man born of woman can harm him. He is warned against Macduff who has fled, so he has his family slaughtered.

When an avenging army invades Scotland, Macbeth sees Birnam Wood—troops using branches as camouflage—moving towards his castle. He rouses himself, but fights against Macduff who tells him he was not born but 'untimely ripp'd' from his mother's womb. Macbeth is killed.

This soldier poet—for his verse is some of the finest Shakespeare ever wrote—grows more impressive as his crimes increase. Finally, he has 'supp'd full with horrors' and 'almost forgot the taste of fears' and reaches a point of bleak, stoical pessimism when life becomes a 'tale told by an idiot, full of sound and fury, signifying nothing'. He has failed to control his destiny and goes down defiantly, fighting like a tiger. This very difficult part has rarely found an actor who is well cast for it, let alone can act it. *Macbeth*

MACBETH, LADY: The powerful, yet ultimately tragic heroine of the play, who banishes her womanhood and all pity to get the throne for her husband. She has to steel him to kill King Duncan. She has decided that the King must be removed before Macbeth even arrives back at Glamis, and, after the murder, incriminates the servants, whose daggers have been used, because his nerve has gone. At the banquet, after Macbeth has become King it is she who saves the situation when he goes to pieces after seeing Banquo's Ghost. But even this cold villainess is finally overtaken by conscience, thus showing she is no female Iago, for in her famous sleepwalking scene she tries to wash away the blood she thinks is on her hands. By now insane from terror and guilt, her death is reported to Macbeth. Her devotion to her husband and the remorse that lies beneath her steely surface, make the part a great one. *Macbeth*

MACDUFF: The Thane of Fife. He discovers the murdered King Duncan and suspects Macbeth, refusing to attend his Coronation or his banquet. He leaves Scotland to join the dead King's son, Malcolm, in England, but is suspected of being a spy of the usurper. The tragic news of his wife and children's murders by Macbeth clears him. He returns to Scotland with Malcolm where he meets Macbeth in battle. The witches have told Macbeth that 'none of woman born' can harm him, but Macduff tells him that he was 'untimely ripp'd' from the womb, then kills him. *Macbeth*

MACDUFF, LADY: Macduff's wife. When he flees to England after Duncan's death, Macbeth orders that she and her children be killed. Her son is killed in front of her and she is killed off-stage. *Macbeth*

MACMORRIS: An Irish officer with the English army. At Harfleur he quarrels with Fluellen. *Henry V*

MALCOLM: Duncan's elder son. The King proclaims him his heir and also Prince of Cumberland. When Duncan is murdered, Malcolm flees to England and his brother, Donalbain, to Ireland and they are at first suspected of the crime. Malcolm returns to Scotland with an avenging army which defeats Macbeth, and he is hailed as king. *Macbeth*

MALVOLIO: Olivia's vain, overbearing, hypocritical and humourless steward. He upsets the drunken Sir Toby, Olivia's servant, Maria, and the simple Sir Andrew, so Maria, abetted by them, Feste, the jester, and Fabian, concocts a plot whereby he will find a letter, apparently from Olivia, commanding him to make love to her. Malvolio swallows the bait, turns up as the letter requests wearing yellow stockings and cross-garters, and makes such a fool of himself that Olivia thinks him mad.

He is locked up in a darkened room and tormented by Feste disguised as Sir Topas the priest. All is finally explained to Olivia, but her steward leaves the house swearing to be revenged on the whole pack of them. Now, his final scenes are sometimes played almost as tragedy, and for sympathy, but there is no reason to suppose that Shakespeare's audiences though him anything but a figure ripe for mocking. *Twelfth Night*

MAMILLIUS: The young son of Leontes and Hermione. When his father's devastating jealousy leads him to accuse his mother of unfaithfulness, the boy is taken from her. When Leontes will not even believe the Oracle's statement that she is innocent, Mamillius dies from sheer fear at her plight. *The Winter's Tale*

MARCELLUS: An officer who has seen the Ghost of Hamlet's father twice on the battlements with Bernardo. They bring Horatio to see it, then tell Hamlet of what they have seen. When he has spoken with his father, he swears Marcellus and Horatio to secrecy. *Hamlet*

MARCH, EARL OF: *see* Mortimer

MARCIUS: The hero's son. When Coriolanus has marched on Rome the boy is taken by Volumnia, his grandmother, and Virgilia, his mother, to beg him to spare the city. *Coriolanus*

MARCUS ANDRONICUS: Titus's brother and a tribune of Rome. He welcomes Titus back from the wars and later finds Titus's daughter, Lavinia, after Demetrius and Chiron have raped and mutilated her. He brings her to Titus and when they discover who the culprits are, swears revenge on them and all their enemies. When this has been done, he tells the people the story of the misfortunes of the Andronici. *Titus Andronicus*

MARDIAN: A eunuch who serves Cleopatra. She sends him to Antony after their defeat to tell him that she has killed herself. *Antony and Cleopatra*

MARGARELON: A bastard son of King Priam. In the battle at the end he challenges Thersites to fight, who refuses, being a bastard like himself, in a witty speech. Margarelon is not amused and exits cursing. *Troilus and Cressida*

MARGARET: Hero's gentlewoman and a witty woman who, without meaning to, helps bring about the downfall of her mistress. She loves Borachio, a follower of the villainous Don John. She agrees, not realizing the implication, to lean out of Hero's window while Borachio makes love to her, calling her Hero. Claudio, Hero's husband-to-be and Don Pedro, are watching and assume that Hero is unfaithful. Borachio later confesses, but says that Margaret is innocent. Her wit gains Benedick's admiration: he says it is 'as quick as the greyhound's mouth'. *Much Ado About Nothing*

MARGARET, QUEEN (MARGARET OF ANJOU): This 'fairest beauty' is captured by Suffolk who falls in love with her, but, being married, decides she must marry Henry—and be his mistress. She is attracted to him. *1 Henry VI*. She is now married to Henry. She dislikes the ambitious Duchess of Gloucester and has her banished for sorcery. She arranges for Suffolk to have Gloucester killed, then, when Suffolk is banished, openly admits she loves him. He, too, is murdered, and she makes her grief plain to Henry. With the Wars of the Roses imminent, York calls her a 'blood-bespotted Neapolitan'. At St. Albans she is forced to flee with Henry. *2 Henry VI*
Henry makes her enemy York his heir instead of their son, Edward, so she raises an army. She defeats York at Wakefield, captures him, crowns him with a paper crown and helps kill him. York's sons defeat her at Towton and she flees to France, where Warwick joins her. They return and she is defeated at Tewkesbury where she is captured and has to watch her son, Edward, killed by Edward IV,

Gloucester and Clarence. 'O kill me too!' she says, but she is ransomed by her father. *3 Henry VI*

She appears (unhistorically) to curse Gloucester memorably—'Thou elvish-mark'd, abortive, rooting hog!' etc. She warns Buckingham against 'younder dog', curses Gloucester and his minions yet again, and goes. On her final appearance, still 'hungry for revenge', and enjoying the 'waning' of her enemies, she is reconciled in her misery with the unhappy Elizabeth, widow of her old enemy, Edward IV. *Richard III*

Margaret's influence on the plays is immense, for her fatal marriage to Henry makes the already inflamed situation worse. York speaks of her 'tiger's heart wrapped in a woman's hide', but the scramble for power has ensured many tigers in the jungle.

MARIA: One of the Princess of France's ladies. Visiting Navarre, they meet the King and his companions who have officially forsworn the company of women for a time. Longaville, one of the King's lords, falls in love with her and she with him, and at the play's end she promises that she will marry him if he will wait a year for her. *Love's Labour's Lost*

Olivia's gentlewoman and a lively, witty member of her household. When the pompous, humourless Malvolio upsets Sir Toby, Sir Andrew and herself, it is she who devises the plot for his downfall, a love-letter, supposed to come from Olivia, that tells him to make love to her. She writes the letter herself in Olivia's hand, and when he declares himself, suggests to her mistress that he is mad. It is also her idea to make Feste, the jester, disguise himself as the curate, Sir Topas, and torment the imprisoned Malvolio. As for Sir Toby, he is so pleased with her scheme, that he finally marries her. *Twelfth Night*

MARIANA: A friend of Diana's mother. She has some strong comments to make on the subject of Bertram and warns Diana against his 'filthy' companion Parolles. *All's Well that Ends Well*

She has been jilted by the hypocritical Angelo when her dowry disappeared in a shipwreck. When Angelo agrees to spare Claudio if his sister, Isabella, gives herself to him, the Duke makes Mariana take her place, unbeknown to Angelo. Angelo still arranges to have Claudio killed and the Duke later orders him to marry Mariana, then that he should be executed. He relents, and Mariana gains her longed-for but—to the rest of us—unattractive spouse. *Measure for Measure*

MARINA: The hero's daughter. She is born at sea and her mother is wrongly thought to have died in childbirth. Pericles leaves her to be brought up at Tarsus by the governor Cleon and his evil wife, Dionyza. The latter arranges for her to be murdered as she surpasses her own daughter, but pirates capture her and take her to a Mytilene brothel where her radiant goodness practically bankrupts the establishment.

The local governor, Lysimachus, a regular, is so overcome by her that he promises to protect her, and her keepers are so tired of her that they place her in a respectable house where she teaches music and needlework. When Lysimachus is visited by Pericles, who thinks his daughter is dead, he orders her to cheer him up by singing. He realizes that she is his daughter and the two are movingly reunited. At the end she is betrothed to Lysimachus.

Marina was adored by those Victorians who dared comment on such a vice-ridden play and has been attacked by more modern commentators as too good to be true. This seems unfair, as she is sympathetic, and her goodness is a key factor in the plot. *Pericles*

MARINER: He takes Antigonus and the infant Perdita to Bohemia. The Mariner warns Antigonus of an approaching storm and that the 'place is famous for the beasts of prey that keep upon't!' *The Winter's Tale*

MARTEXT, SIR OLIVER: A vicar who is just about to marry Touchstone and Audrey when Jacques tells them to go to church and find a good priest. To his annoyance, they do so. *As You Like It*

MARTIUS: One of Titus's four sons. He and his brother Quintus fall into a pit where the sons of Queen Tamora have thrown the body of Bassianus. They are accused of having murdered him and are put to death. *Titus Andronicus*

MARULLUS: *see* Flavius

MASTER: One of a gang of pirates who capture Suffolk. He is given a prisoner as booty. *2 Henry VI*

MASTER-GUNNER OF ORLEANS: He aims his gun at a secret window used by the English to spy on the city. His son fires it and the shot kills Salisbury and Sir Thomas Gargrave. *1 Henry VI*

MASTER OF A SHIP: Captain of the ship wrecked by Prospero's magic. *The Tempest*

MASTER'S MATE: One of the pirates who capture Suffolk and is offered a share in the booty. *2 Henry VI*

MAYOR OF ST. ALBANS: He presents an allegedly blind man called Simpcox to the King. Gloucester exposes him as a fraud and tells the Mayor to send for a whip. *2 Henry VI*

MAYOR OF YORK: He is talked into yielding up the keys of the city to Edward IV. *3 Henry VI*

MECAENAS: A friend of Octavius. He asks Enobarbus about Cleopatra, which leads to his famous description of her. He appears in later scenes without saying much. *Antony and Cleopatra*

MELUN: French Count, whose 'grandsire was an Englishman', is brought mortally wounded to Salisbury and Pembroke. He warns them that when they have helped the Dauphin defeat John they will be beheaded. *King John*

MENAS: A pirate and a friend of Pompey. When Antony, Octavius and Lepidus are feasting in Pompey's ship,

Menas asks him if he would be lord of all the world and suggests cutting the cable and letting him 'fall to the throats' of all three. Pompey tells him he should have done it, not spoken about it. *Antony and Cleopatra*

MENECRATES: A friend of Pompey and a pirate. He appears briefly as his adviser. *Antony and Cleopatra*

MENELAUS: A Greek general and the husband of Helen, who has deserted him for Paris, bringing about the Trojan War. Though he appears a number of times he has little to say. He fights Paris to a ribald commentary from Thersites. *Troilus and Cressida*

MENENIUS AGRIPPA: An elderly patrician and friend of Coriolanus. He prevents a rebellion of the plebians, convincing them of the patricians' care of them, and telling them a fable about the members of the body rebelling against the belly. He works on Coriolanus to prevent his showing his contempt of the plebs when asking to be confirmed as Consul. When Coriolanus so enrages the citizens that they want him killed, Menenius calms them by saying he will bring him to answer them, but Coriolanus refuses until his mother asks him. After his banishment and subsequent march on Rome, Menenius has sardonic remarks to make to those that banished him. He pleads with Coriolanus to spare the city, but he will not listen. He later rejoices to hear that Coriolanus's family have made him change his mind. *Coriolanus*

MENTIETH: A Scottish noble who fights with Malcolm against Macbeth. *Macbeth*

MERCADE: At the height of the revelry, he brings the Princess news of her father's death in a few electric exchanges with her. The best minute part in Shakespeare. *Love's Labour's Lost*

MERCUTIO: Romeo's witty, fiery-tempered friend who dominates the play until his death. This Renaissance Man, one of the very finest secondary rôles in Shakespeare, first appears with Romeo and Benvolio on his way to the Capulet's ball. Romeo's lovelorn state over his Rosaline triggers off the scintillating Queen Mab speech from Mercutio. After the ball he laughingly tries to find Romeo who by now has fallen in love with Juliet. In a Verona street he and Benvolio meet him again and tease him in a bravura manner, then bawdily tease the Nurse.

In his final scene, Mercutio and Benvolio are accosted by the 'spitfire' Tybalt, Juliet's cousin. Romeo enters and refuses to fight Tybalt because of his love for Juliet, so Mercutio takes up the quarrel. Romeo tries to part them and this helps to bring about Mercutio's death. 'A plague on both your houses!' he laments, puncturing his own wit even in death. The part rivals Hotspur as an actor's dream. *Romeo and Juliet*

MESSALA: A friend of Brutus and Cassius. He brings Brutus news that Cicero has been executed and that his wife, Portia, is dead. After Brutus's death, Messala joins Octavius Caesar. *Julius Caesar*

METELLUS CIMBER: *see* Cimber, Metellus

MICHAEL: One of Cade's rebels. *2 Henry VI*

MICHAEL, SIR: A friend of the Archbishop of York who sends him to the Lord Marshal and his cousin, Scroop, with dispatches. *1 Henry IV*

MILAN, DUKE OF: Silvia's father, who wishes her to marry Thurio though she loves Valentine. The Duke banishes Valentine when Proteus, the other 'gentleman', treacherously tells him that Valentine is going to elope with Silvia. She follows him, and the Duke and Thurio follow her and are seized by outlaws. Their captain is now Valentine who releases the Duke and gains Silvia, when Thurio, like a coward, will not fight for her. *The Two Gentlemen of Verona*

MIRANDA: The heroine, and Prospero's daughter. She has lived on Prospero's island since infancy and never met another man. She falls in love with the shipwrecked

Ferdinand soon after Prospero tells her how he and she came to be on the island. To test Ferdinand, Prospero pretends to suspect him and enslaves him. Miranda begs him to let her help him to pile logs. He passes the test, the two are betrothed and a masque is performed for them. Ferdinand's father later sees them playing chess. The pair set out to be married in Naples. Miranda is a sweet, kindly girl, innocently ignorant of the world. *The Tempest*

MONTAGUE: Romeo's father and the enemy of the Capulets. In the first scene he is spoiling for a fight with old Capulet and later questions Benvolio about Romeo. He appears again after Mercutio's and Tybalt's deaths and Romeo's banishment, and at the end, with Romeo and Juliet dead, settles his quarrel with Capulet, saying he will erect a golden statue to Juliet. *Romeo and Juliet*

MONTAGUE, LADY: Romeo's mother. She speaks in the opening scene, trying to restrain her husband, appears again after Romeo's banishment and is reported by Montague at the end to have died of grief. *Romeo and Juliet*

MONTAGUE, MARQUESS OF: A Yorkist, who, with his brother, Warwick, changes sides when Edward IV marries Lady Grey and is killed with him at Barnet. *3 Henry VI*

MONTANO: The governor of Cyprus before Othello. He tries to stop Roderigo fighting the drunken Cassio and is wounded by the latter. After Desdemona's death, Montano disarms Othello, puts him under guard and goes to arrest Iago. *Othello*

MONTGOMERY, SIR JOHN: A Yorkist who urges Edward, when he returns from Burgundy, to become King. *3 Henry VI*

MONTJOY: The chief French herald. Before Agincourt he twice demands that Henry pays ransom to compensate for the damage and deaths he has caused, but after the battle he humbly admits defeat. He tells the King the field is called Agincourt. *Henry V*

MOPSA: A shepherdess who first quarrels with Dorcas over the Clown, then dances and sings with her and Autolycus. *The Winter's Tale*

MORGAN: The name the banished Belarius takes as a disguise. *Cymbeline*

MOROCCO, PRINCE OF: A dusky and unsuccessful suitor of Portia who, in the casket test, chooses the golden one. *The Merchant of Venice*

MORTIMER, EDMUND, EARL OF MARCH: Captured by Glendower, he has married his daughter. His sister is Hotspur's wife. In Mortimer's one scene the three men optimistically divide England and Wales into three parts before the rebellion. *1 Henry IV*

An old man in the Tower who claims he should be king and names his nephew, Richard Plantaganet, as his heir. The nephew of the above, confused by Shakespeare with him. *1 Henry VI*

MORTIMER, LADY: Mortimer's Welsh wife and Owen Glendower's daughter. She speaks and sings in Welsh. *1 Henry IV*

MORTIMER, SIR JOHN AND SIR HUGH: Uncles and supporters of York, who are killed at Wakefield. *3 Henry VI*

MORTON: He brings Northumberland news of Hotspur's death at Shrewsbury. *2 Henry IV*

See Ely, Bishop of

MOTH: Don Armado's bright, witty and pert page, with him in his scenes. He is cast as the infant Hercules in the 'Interlude of the Nine Worthies'. *Love's Labour's Lost*

One of Titania's fairies who attends Bottom. *A Midsummer Night's Dream*

MOULDY, RALPH: He is pressed to serve with Falstaff but is worries about how his 'old dame' will get on and pays Bardolph forty shillings for his release. *2 Henry IV*

MOWBRAY, LORD: Having joined the rebellion of Scroop and Hastings, he and they are persuaded by Prince John to dismiss their men, then treacherously arrested and executed. *2 Henry IV*

MOWBRAY, THOMAS, DUKE OF NORFOLK: Father of the above. Bolingbroke accuses him of stealing royal funds and murdering the King's uncle, Gloucester, and Richard banishes him for life. He is later reported dead. *Richard II*

MURDERERS: They appear in several plays. Two are hired by Suffolk to kill Gloucester. *2 Henry VI*

Two more memorable and choice ones kill Clarence after being hired by Richard personally, the second one later displaying qualms at the deed. *Richard III*

Murderers dispatch Banquo and Macduff's family. *Macbeth.* (Is the 3rd Murderer of Banquo Macbeth himself?)

MUSTARD-SEED: One of Titania's fairies who attends Bottom. *A Midsummer Night's Dream*

MUTIUS: Titus's youngest son. His father kills him when Bassianus carries off Lavinia, Mutius's sister, and the youth tries to stop Titus interfering. *Titus Andronicus*

N

NATHANIEL, SIR: A curate and a friend of Holofernes the schoolmaster, whom he much admires. In the 'Interlude of the Nine Worthies', performed for the courtiers, Nathaniel plays Alexander, but is so mocked by Berowne that he has to abandon his rôle, being, as Costard says, 'a foolish mild man . . . and soon dashed'. He is also a 'marvellous good neighbour' and a very good bowler! *Love's Labour's Lost*

NATHANIEL: A servant of Petruchio. *The Taming of the Shrew*

NERISSA: Portia's waiting-maid and confidante. She falls in love with and marries Gratiano, then, when Portia disguises herself as a lawyer to save Antonio, Nerissa becomes a lawyer's clerk. Gratiano gives up his wedding ring to the 'clerk' for his services in helping get Antonio acquitted, and later has some explaining to do to Nerissa. *The Merchant of Venice*

NESTOR: A wise, old Greek commander. He joins Ulysses in a plan to rouse Achilles from inaction by suggesting to the idle hero that Ajax is a worthier man. Nestor goes to Troy to demand that Helen be given up or else the war will drag on, then joins Ulysses in boosting the ego of the simple Ajax. After this he plays no key part in the action until he orders the dead body of Achilles' friend, Patroclus, to be carried to him, which has the desired effect. *Troilus and Cressida*

NORFOLK, THOMAS MOWBRAY, DUKE OF: *see* Mowbray. *Richard II*

NORFOLK, JOHN MOWBRAY, 3RD DUKE OF: A Yorkist supporter, appearing briefly in two scenes. *3 Henry VI*

NORFOLK, JOHN HOWARD, 1ST DUKE OF: He and his son, Surrey, have 'the leading of this foot and horse' at Bosworth. He finds a message on his tent reading: 'Jockey of Norfolk, be not too bold, for Dickon thy master is bought and sold' and shows it to the King, who says it is a thing devised by the enemy. In the battle Norfolk is killed. *Richard III*

NORFOLK, THOMAS HOWARD, 2ND DUKE OF: He appears as Surrey and fights at Bosworth. *Richard III*. He appears in the first scene as a bitter opponent of Wolsey, whom he discusses with Buckingham and others, and later rejoices at the downfall of the 'little good Cardinal'. He is in Anne's Coronation procession and at the infant Elizabeth's christening. *Henry VIII*

NORFOLK, THOMAS HOWARD, 3RD DUKE OF: As Surrey (q.v.), he appears as son of the above. *Henry VIII*

NORTHUMBERLAND, HENRY PERCY, EARL OF: He takes Bolingbroke's side against the 'degenerate' king and acts as the former's messenger at Flint Castle. A much less attractive character than his son, Hotspur, he enjoys tormenting Richard in the deposition scene until the unfortunate king shouts 'Fiend! thou torment'st me ere I come to hell.' Bolingbroke makes Northumberland stop. When he later tells Richard he must go to Pomfret, not the Tower, Richard warns him that his greed and ambition will lead to his downfall. *Richard II*
He agrees to rebel against the King with his son and his brother Worcester because of Henry's ingratitude, but fails to appear at the Battle of Shrewsbury, pretending to be ill. *1 Henry IV*
He hears of Hotspur's death, then leads Archbishop Scroop of York to think he will support another rebellion, but flees to Scotland instead. There he is defeated. *2 Henry IV*

NORTHUMBERLAND, EARL OF: Hotspur's grandson and a Lancastrian supporter. In the nightmarish scene where the captured York is butchered, only Northumberland, moved by York's speech, shows pity for him. He is killed at Towton. *3 Henry VI*

NORTHUMBERLAND, LADY: The Earl's wife who persuades him to fly to Scotland rather than rebel again. *2 Henry IV*

NURSE: Juliet's nurse, and a major comic creation. Her name is Angelica. Talkative, bawdy, affectionate and cynical, she first encourages Juliet to marry Paris, but when she finds her beloved Juliet has fallen in love with Romeo, consents to act as go-between. Shaken by the death of her friend, Tybalt, she later urges Juliet to forget Romeo who has killed him and marry Paris, but she agrees to go to Friar Laurence's cell, where he is hiding after his banishment. However, she later tells Juliet to forget him once more. It is she who finds Juliet apparently dead, after which she vanishes from the play. Doctor Johnson summed her up as 'at once loquacious and secret, obsequious and insolent, trusty and dishonest'. *Romeo and Juliet*

She witnesses the birth of the villainous Tamara's child by the equally villainous Aaron. When she brings him his offspring, he kills her to keep the birth a secret. *Titus Andronicus*

NYM: He keeps using the words 'humour' or 'humours'. Some have thought him a caricature of Ben Jonson. Falstaff tells him to take a love letter to Mrs. Ford, but he will not perform such a 'base humour', so is dismissed, along with Pistol. In revenge, they tell Ford and Page about Falstaff's letters to their wives. *The Merry Wives of Windsor* In *Henry V* he is a corporal. He quarrels with his betrothed, Mistress Quickly, who marries Pistol instead. He then quarrels with him, but they go off to France together to the wars, along with Bardolph. They become experts in looting and Bardolph and Nym are hanged for it.

O

OBERON: King of the Fairies. He quarrels with Titania over a 'little changeling boy' whom he wants as a page. So he decides to humiliate her by having Puck put a magic potion on her eyes which will make her fall in love with the first living creature she sees when she wakes. She sees Bottom 'translated' into an ass. He also has Puck put the potion on Demetrius to make him fall in love with Helena. After this has led to complications, all is finally resolved, with each pair of the Athenian lovers correctly paired off. Oberon then releases Titania from her spell and he and his queen prepare to dance at the marriage of Theseus and Hippolyta. *A Midsummer Night's Dream*

OCTAVIA: Octavius Caesar's sister, who is married to Antony as a political move to improve relations between the two men. He deserts her to return to Cleopatra. *Antony and Cleopatra*

OCTAVIUS: *see* Caesar, Octavius

OLD LADY: She has a pleasant, teasing scene with Anne Bullen. Later, she tells the King he has a daughter and gets given a hundred marks. *Henry VIII*

OLD MAN: A tenant of Gloucester who guides him across the heath after he is blinded. *King Lear*

OLIVER: The eldest son of Sir Rowland de Boys. He envies his brother, Orlando, and arranges for Charles the Wrestler to break his neck. Instead, Charles is beaten and Orlando flees into the forest. Duke Frederick orders Oliver to bring him back. He follows his brother who saves him from a snake and a lioness. After this, Oliver repents to the extent of giving his estate to Orlando. Oliver and Rosalind's companion, Celia, fall in love and are married. *As You Like It*

OLIVIA: A rich, young Illyrian countess. We meet her mourning excessively for her dead brother, and determined to reject the suit of the Duke Orsino who is in love with her. To her comes the Duke's messenger, Cesario, actually Viola in disguise. Olivia promptly falls passionately in love with 'him', and makes her devotion plain.
Meanwhile, her kinsman, Sir Toby, her maid, Maria, and her jester, Feste, make her pompous steward, Malvolio, believe that she is in love with him, and he ludicrously comes to pay court, to her amazement. She orders that he be taken care of. She meets Sebastian, Viola's identical twin, and rushes the startled youth to a wedding ceremony. Then she meets Viola, addresses her as her husband, and is beside herself with frustration and fury until Sebastian appears and all is explained. Malvolio, who has been imprisoned by Sir Toby and his friends, is brought in, and

Olivia explains that she knew nothing of the plot against him. *Twelfth Night*

OPHELIA: Polonius's daughter and Laertes's sister, who loves Hamlet. We first meet her saying goodbye to Laertes, who is on his way back to school, and who warns her not to believe Hamlet's protestations of love. Her father tells her the same thing. She later tells him how she has been frightened by Hamlet, who is pretending to be mad. Polonius arranges for her to meet Hamlet while he and the King spy on them. Hamlet orders her to get to a nunnery and savagely denounces both women and marriage. 'O! what a noble mind is here o'erthrown,' she laments. During the play scene he sits and flirts with her. The next time we meet her, she has gone mad, and her famous mad scene is punctuated with haunting snatches of song. She wanders away and drowns herself. *Hamlet*

ORLANDO: The youngest son of Sir Rowland de Boys and the play's hero. His brother, Oliver, has deliberately prevented him being educated properly. They quarrel and Oliver arranges for Duke Frederick's wrestler to kill Orlando. However, Orlando emerges the winner and, with his faithful old servant, Adam, escapes to the Forest of Arden, having, in the meantime, met and fallen in love with Rosalind. There he finds the banished Duke who welcomes him and Adam after Orlando has broken in upon his party demanding food. He proceeds to decorate the trees with poems about his beloved Rosalind, who has fled to the forest disguised as a youth, Ganymede. He meets her but does not recognize her. She says she can cure him of his love if he woos her by pretending she is Rosalind, and she conducts the mock wooing with much wit and teasing.

Oliver now comes to the forest to catch Orlando. He falls asleep and Orlando saves him from a lioness and a snake. Oliver repents and offers Orlando his estate. Rosalind appears dressed as a woman and the lovers are truly reunited. *As You Like It*

ORLEANS, BASTARD OF: He introduces Joan la Pucelle (Joan of Arc) to the Dauphin, believing in her power to drive out the English. He enters Orleans with Joan, but the French are driven out in their shirts. He is with her when she captures Rouen for a short time. At Bordeaux he wants the bodies of Talbot and his son hacked to pieces. *1 Henry VI*

ORLEANS, CHARLES, DUKE OF: He defends his cousin, the Dauphin's, reputation for courage when the Constable of France casts doubts on it. He also sneers at Henry and his followers and boasts that at Agincourt he and his companions will 'have each a hundred Englishmen'. He is captured in the battle. *Henry V*

ORSINO: The Duke of Illyria, wallowing in his melancholy condition as the rejected suitor of Olivia. In the very first speech of the play—'If music be the food of love, play on . . .'—he shows how much he enjoys the rôle. He takes a liking to Viola, disguised as the page, Cesario, and sends her to do his wooing, as he cannot get himself admitted to see her. Meanwhile, Viola falls in love with Orsino. At the end of the play when the complications of the plot have been put straight, he realizes that he cannot get Olivia and decides to make Viola 'Orsino's mistress and his fancy's queen'. *Twelfth Night*

OSRIC: A foppish courtier, who appears in the last act. He welcomes Hamlet back to Denmark and tells him that Claudius has wagered that Hamlet will defeat Laertes in the duel they are to fight. He is in charge of the fencing match, and it is to him that Laertes confesses his treachery before he dies. The part is a gem. *Hamlet*

OSWALD: Goneril's devoted servant. He insults Lear and gets tripped up by Kent, and later beaten up by him. On his way from his mistress to Edmund, carrying a love-letter, he comes across the blinded Gloucester and is about to kill him when he is himself killed by Edgar. From remarks made by Edgar, Oswald may well have been Goneril's lover. *King Lear*

OTHELLO: A Moorish general in the service of Venice and the play's tragic hero. First seen as a noble, trusting, proud figure, he is brought down by the malignant Iago and his own catastrophic jealousy. His greatest admirers have believed him a flawless hero; some modern critics, including T. S. Eliot and F. R. Leavis, have found him proud to the point of arrogance, a self-idealist, self-dramatizing his situation.

His ensign, Iago, hates him for making Cassio his lieutenant instead of him. Othello having secretly married Brabantio's daughter, Desdemona, is summoned to the Duke because the Turks are sailing on Cyprus. In the Council Chamber, Brabantio accuses him of bewitching his daughter, but Othello eloquently describes how she came to love him, and she declares her love. Othello is made Governor of Cyprus and Brabantio is reluctantly forced to accept the match.

The Turks are scattered by a storm. Othello arrives in Cyprus to greet his 'fair warrior', who has been escorted there by Iago. General rejoicing is proclaimed to celebrate the marriage, but Othello is forced to dismiss Cassio who has been made drunk by Iago and become involved in an engineered brawl. Iago continues his work of destruction by having Cassio ask Desdemona to intercede with Othello. Overwhelmed by his love which can deny her nothing, he says he will consider it, but Iago starts to rouse Othello's suspicions that the pair are lovers. At first, he will not believe him, but in a supreme scene, 'honest' Iago plays Othello along, the Moor bidding farewell to his 'tranquil mind'. He turns on Iago with 'Villain, be sure thou prove my love a whore', but is soon being tricked by Iago until he is howling for blood and swearing an oath of vengeance with him.

Iago gets hold of a handkerchief which Othello has given Desdemona and which she has dropped. He arranges that Cassio finds it and that Othello sees him with it. After going into an epileptic fit, Othello is finally convinced of her guilt. Now he is prepared to 'chop her into messes' because she has betrayed *him*.

Letters from Venice recall Othello and name Cassio his deputy. He strikes Desdemona publicly when she has hoped the breach between him and Cassio may be healed, later rails against her savagely and says he mistook her for the 'cunning whore of Venice'. He goes to her bedchamber, wakes her to tell her she must pray and die, and smothers her. Emilia, her servant and Iago's wife, breaks in and calls for help. Othello learns the truth, tries to kill Iago and in a great final speech, in which he says he has loved 'not wisely but too well', stabs himself and dies over Desdemona's body. 'He was great of heart' says the wronged Cassio as if in answer to critics who find even this final speech self-dramatizing. *Othello*

OUTLAWS: They capture Valentine in a forest and make him their general. The Duke later pardons them. *The Two Gentlemen of Verona*

OVERDONE, MISTRESS: A bawd who keeps a brothel. The strict morality laws now in force in Venice are doing her trade no good, as if the wars, poverty and the gallows are not enough. She gets sent to prison. We learn from Pompey that she has had nine husbands, being 'Overdone by the last'. *Measure for Measure*

OXFORD, EARL OF: A Lancastrian. In France he criticizes Warwick for betraying Henry and reminds him that his own father and brother have been killed by Edward IV. *3 Henry VI*. He is one of Richmond's supporters at Bosworth. *Richard III*

P

PAGE: He appears in the Induction and is made by the Lord to disguise himself as a woman and pretend to be the wife of Sly the tinker. His name is Bartholomew. *The Taming of the Shrew*

PAGE, ANNE: The daughter of the Pages. Her father wants her to marry Slender, her mother, Dr. Caius, while she loves Fenton. She elopes with him and, when they are faced with the facts, her parents forgive her. *The Merry Wives of Windsor*

PAGE, MASTER GEORGE: Anne's father, and a gentleman of Windsor. He is called Thomas in one scene. Nym tells him that Falstaff means to seduce his wife, but he does not doubt her, unlike the jealous Ford who suspects the worst of his wife. Page tells Ford to trust Mrs. Ford. His attitude to his daughter's marriage is noted above. *The Merry Wives of Windsor*

PAGE, MISTRESS MEG: Master Page's wife and one of the 'merry wives'. Like Mistress Ford, she receives a love letter from Falstaff, and the two combine to humiliate him. She thinks up the scheme for baiting the fat knight in Windsor Forest. Her attitude to Anne's marriage is noted above, and it is she who brings her husband round to accepting Fenton. *The Merry Wives of Windsor*

PAGE, WILLIAM: Anne's young brother. Sir Hugh Evans, the parson, tests his knowledge of Latin out rather stupidly, which leads to some villainous punning by Mistress Quickly. Evans is pleased with the lad. *The Merry Wives of Windsor*

PAGE TO FALSTAFF: *see* Boy

PANDAR: He owns a brothel in Mytilene. Worried by being 'too Wenchless', he tells Boult to search for some. He returns with the play's heroine, Marina, who is not only a steadfast virgin, but starts ruining the Pandar's business by reforming his patrons. He is an unhappy man. *Pericles*

PANDARUS: Cressida's uncle and the go-between for her and Troilus. In his bawdy way he is genuinely fond of the lovers, being more of an aunt to Cressida, gossip and all, than an uncle. He characterizes the Trojans to Cressida as they watch them returning from battle, and he later tells her she is to be exchanged for Antenor. Troilus sees she is unfaithful and he rounds savagely on Pandarus who laments the lot of go-betweens. *Troilus and Cressida*

PANDULPH: A cardinal and the Papal Legate who excommunicates John and urges the French to go to war with him. He later tells the Dauphin to claim the English throne in the name of his wife, Blanch. John submits to Pandulph, who says he will now stop the war, but the Dauphin refuses to listen. *King John*

PANTHINO: Antonio's servant. Panthino urges him to send his son, Proteus, to Milan, after talking to Antonio's brother about the matter. Then he sees to it that Proteus and his servant, Launce, catch the boat. *The Two Gentlemen of Verona*

PAROLLES: A despicable crony of the play's unlikable hero, Bertram, who at first does not see Parolles for what he is, 'a vile rascal', 'notorious liar', coward, braggart and, in the memorable words of Lafeu, a 'general offence'. Yet he is an amusing knave, and the part is a good one.

We meet him arguing the merits of virginity with Helena, the heroine. He goes to Paris with Bertram and, when the latter is made to marry Helena by the King who has been cured by her, Parolles encourages Bertram to go to Florence and the wars. In Italy, his bragging and cowardice so anger his fellow officers that they pretend to be the enemy, capture him, speak in a strange tongue and take him to Bertram, who hears him give away to an 'interpreter' all the secrets he can remember about the French army. Bertram wants him whipped round the army, but Parolles pleads for his life so effectively and shamelessly that he is spared and resolves cheerfully to give up soldiering and live in shame and folly. He returns to Court, helps unravel the plot, and looks set fair for the future. *All's Well that Ends Well*

PATIENCE: A gentlewoman of Queen Katharine who attends her when she is dying. *Henry VIII*

PATROCLUS: One of the Greek commanders and a close friend of Achilles, being called his 'masculine whore' by Thersites. Though he tells Agamemnon that Achilles will not fight, he later tries to persuade him to take the field. Not until Hector kills Patroclus will Achilles rouse himself to combat. *Troilus and Cressida*

PAULINA: The wife of Antigonus and lady-in-waiting of Queen Hermione, whom she fiercely defends when King Leontes accuses her of being unfaithful. She brings Leontes the infant, Perdita, who is banished and taken to a desert spot by her husband who is eaten by a bear there. She tells Leontes of Hermione's apparent death, and sixteen years later, she arranges the display of the statue of Hermione to Leontes, which turns out to be Hermione herself. The King suggests that the 'good Paulina' shall marry Camillo. *The Winter's Tale*

PEASEBLOSSOM: One of Titania's fairies commanded to serve Bottom. *A Midsummer Night's Dream*

PEDANT: Tranio, pretending to be his master, Lucentio, frightens the Pedant, who happens to look like Lucentio's father, Vincentio, into pretending to be the old man. The Pedant later tries to have the real Vincentio arrested as a madman, but escapes when the plot is revealed. However, he is at the final banquet. *The Taming of the Shrew*

PEDRO, DON: The Prince of Aragon. This pleasant ruler has defeated his bastard brother, John, and goes to visit Leonato at Messina with his apparently reconciled brother and his followers, Claudio and Benedick. He woos Leonato's daughter, Hero, for Claudio and is a leader in the plot to make Benedick think that Beatrice loves him. Meanwhile, he is deceived, like Claudio, into thinking Hero is unfaithful, by a plot of John's. When the plot is revealed, he is appalled and is most anxious to make amends. An honest, attractive nobleman. *Much Ado About Nothing*

PEMBROKE, WILLIAM HERBERT, EARL OF: A Yorkist who is ordered by Edward IV to levy men. *3 Henry VI*

PEMBROKE, WILLIAM MARSHAL, EARL OF: He objects
to the King's submission to the Pope and the imprisonment
of Arthur, whom he later accuses John of murdering. He
(unhistorically) joins the Dauphin who has invaded
England, but when he discovers that he and the other
English lords are to be murdered as soon as the invasion is
successful, he rejoins John. *King John*

PERCY, HENRY: *see* Hotspur, *also see* Northumberland

PERCY, LADY: Hotspur's wife and the sister of Roger
Mortimer. She is a worthy wife for the great Hotspur, being
high-spirited, attractive and amusing. In Part I, she asks
her husband to confide in her about his plans, but he
banteringly refuses. She is with him in Wales where they
are with Glendower, Mortimer and Lady Mortimer. After
the latter has sung in Welsh, Hotspur asks his Kate to sing,
but she refuses. In Part 2, she proudly recalls her dead
husband, and tells Northumberland not to wrong his ghost
by helping other rebels when he did not help his own son.
1 and 2 Henry IV

PERCY, THOMAS: *see* Worcester

PERDITA: The daughter of King Leontes and Queen
Hermione of Sicilia, who is banished as an infant by the
jealous king who wrongly thinks that his wife has been
unfaithful to him with King Polixenes of Bohemia. The baby
is abandoned on the coast of Bohemia where she is found
and brought up by an old shepherd. Sixteen years later she
is a beautiful girl, and Florizel, son of Polixenes, has fallen
in love with her. Polixenes forbids the match, not knowing
her origin. The lovers flee to Sicilia where Leontes and his
daughter are reunited. Polixenes, who follows them, is
reconciled to Leontes, and Perdita meets her mother, who
was thought to have died, but was alive all the time.
Perdita is a delightful character who makes a deep impression on everyone she meets. Florizel says of her: 'when
you do dance, I wish you a wave o' the sea, that you might

do nothing but that . . . All your acts are queens'. *The Winter's Tale*

PERICLES: The Prince of Tyre and the much-afflicted, stoical hero of the play. He goes to Antioch to woo King Antiochus's daughter by solving a riddle. This reveals that father and daughter have committed incest and Pericles is forced to flee for his life when he solves it. He flees from Tyre itself and goes to Tarsus where he saves the citizens from famine by giving them grain.

On the run again, he is shipwrecked and reaches Penta-polis, winning the king's daughter, Thaisa, in a tourna-ment. Hearing that his enemies are dead, he sails for home, but Thaisa apparently dies giving birth to a daughter though she actually survives. Meanwhile, Pericles goes to Tarsus and leaves his infant daughter, Marina, with the governor, Cleon, and his wife, Dionyza. Then he goes to Tyre.

Years later he is told by Cleon and his evil wife that Marina has died: actually, Dionyza has tried to kill her, but she has been taken by pirates. Pericles sees her alleged grave at Tarsus and is struck dumb with grief. Sailing home, he is driven to Mytilene where Marina has been put in a brothel, but has escaped unscathed. Father and daughter are happily reunited, then Pericles is summoned to Ephesus where he and Marina find Thaisa, who has become a high priestess of Diana. *Pericles*

PETER: The Nurse's servant, with her when she meets Mercutio and Benvolio. She upbraids him for letting the bantering pair 'use' her. After Juliet's death, he has a scene with musicians, asking them to play 'Heart's Ease'. *Romeo and Juliet*

PETER OF POMFRET: The King orders him to be im-prisoned and hanged when he prophesies that John will deliver up his crown before Ascension Day. *King John*

PETER THUMP: An apprentice who accuses his master, Thomas Horner, of saying that York should be King. They fight in front of Edward IV with sandbags and Peter kills his drunken master. *2 Henry VI*

PETO: A crony of Falstaff. In Part 1 he helps rob the travellers near Rochester and is robbed in turn by the disguised Prince Hal and Poins. Later, he tells the Prince how Falstaff has hacked his sword with his dagger to suggest he has fought hard. In Part 2, he warns Hal that rebellion has broken out and that Falstaff is wanted. *1 and 2 Henry IV*

PETRUCHIO: The fortune-hunting hero of the play, on the look-out for a rich wife. Hearing about Katharina the Shrew's large dowry, he sets out to woo her, a little to help his friend Hortensio win Bianca, Katharina's sister, whose father insists that Katharina marry first, but mainly for the money.

He arranges a wedding for the next Sunday and despite her saying that she will see him hanged first, brings her to the altar. As soon as he owns her, he takes her to his country house and breaks her spirit by preventing her eating and sleeping, playing practical jokes on her, pretending to be over-solicitous. Finally, when the poor girl agrees that the sun is the moon and that old Vincentio is a pretty young girl, he takes her back to Padua tamed. He, Lucentio and Hortensio each bet that their own wife is the most submissive and Petruchio wins outright. Katharina is a model wife. Petruchio's swaggering and brazen methods hardly make him an ideal hero, but his gusto and common sense make the part a fine one. *The Taming of the Shrew*

PHEBE: A shepherdess who despises her adoring Silvius and falls in love with Ganymede, actually Rosalind in disguise. She sends 'him' a love letter, using the wretched Silvius as messenger. Rosalind says she will marry her if ever she marries woman, but that Phebe must marry Silvius if she finds she cannot marry Ganymede. The scornful girl finds that she has to marry Silvius, when she realizes her beloved is actually a woman. Surprisingly, she accepts the prospect quite gracefully. *As You Like It*

PHILARIO: An Italian, friend and host of the banished Posthumus. He tries to stop Posthumus and Iacho making a wager about Posthumus's wife, Imogen's, chastity. When Iachimo returns from Britain having apparently seduced Imogen and won the bet, Philario urges Posthumus not to believe Iachimo's alleged 'proofs'. *Cymbeline*

PHILEMON: A servant of Cerimon, who sends him to fetch fire and meat for some shipwrecked travellers. *Pericles*

PHILIP, KING OF FRANCE: A supporter of young Arthur's claim to the English crown. He sends an ambassador to demand that John abdicates, which leads to the angry king invading France. Peace comes when John's niece Blanch marries Philip's son, but the papal legate Pandulph threatens Philip with excommunication if he makes an alliance with the 'arch-heretic' John. Philip gives in to Pandulph. In the battle that follows, the French are defeated. He later tries to comfort the desperate Constance, mother of Arthur, who has been captured by John. *King John*

PHILIP THE BASTARD: *see* Faulconbridge

PHILO: A friend of Antony's who only appears—memorably—in the opening scene. In the play's first speech he describes Antony's 'dotage' over Cleopatra—the 'triple pillar of the world transform'd into a strumpet's fool'. *Antony and Cleopatra*

PHILOSTRATE: Master of the Revels at Theseus's court who arranges the celebration of his wedding to Hippolyta. These include the performance by Bottom and company of 'Pyramus and Thisbe', which he tries to prevent because, though only some 'ten words long', it is ten words too long. *A Midsummer Night's Dream*

PHILOTEN: The daughter of Cleon and the evil Dionyza. Though she does not appear, she is important because she is so outshone by Marina, the heroine, that Dionyza decides to have Marina murdered. *Pericles*

PHILOTUS: A servant of one of Timon's creditors who tries to get a debt settled without success. *Timon of Athens*

PHRYNIA: One of Alcibiades' mistresses. Timon rails against her, and she replies: 'Thy lips rot off!' To her delight, he gives her gold as he curses her. *Timon of Athens*

PINCH: A schoolmaster and conjuror. He is urged by Adriana to conjure back Antipholus of Ephesus to his senses. Adriana has mistaken Antipholus for her husband, his twin, Antipholus of Syracuse, and muddled up their twin servants, the Dromios, as well. The mountebank conjuror says Antipholus and Dromio are possessed of the devil and must be locked up in a dark room. *The Comedy of Errors*

PINDARUS: Cassius's servant. He wrongly tells Cassius that his friend Titinius has been captured at Philippi, and Cassius, who knows that the battle is already lost, says he can have his freedom if he kills him with the sword that 'ran through Caesar's bowels'. Pindarus obeys him, then runs away. *Julius Caesar*

PISANIO: Posthumus's servant. When his master is banished, he tells him to serve his wife, Imogen. The faithful Pisanio is later told to kill her by Posthumus who wrongly thinks she is unfaithful. He does not believe it and, on the way to a spot where she thinks she will meet her husband, Pisanio tells her his orders and urges her to disguise herself as a page and enter the Roman Lucius's service. It is Pisanio who reveals the truth of Imogen's identity at the end of the play. *Cymbeline*

PISTOL: Falstaff's 'ancient' (ensign), and a bragging, ranting fraud of an old soldier, who misquotes Marlowe and is thought to be a walking parody of the sort of plays and playing to be found with the Admiral's Men, Shakespeare's main rivals. He brings Falstaff the news that Henry IV is dead, and that his beloved Hal is now king, and goes to London with him, being present when Hal disowns him. When Falstaff is thrown into the Fleet, so is Pistol. *2 Henry IV*

He is still with Falstaff until dismissed for refusing to take a love letter to Mistress Page. He gets his revenge by telling Ford about Falstaff's designs on Mistress Ford. He decides to marry Mistress Quickly and helps in the baiting of Falstaff in Windsor Forest, playing Hobgoblin. *The Merry Wives of Windsor*

He is now married to Mistress Quickly and is Host of the Boar's Head. He listens to his wife's great description of Falstaff's death, then goes off to the French wars with Bardolph and Nym, where his main interest is in thieving and looting. He quarrels with Fluellen who later strikes him and makes him eat a leek. Earlier, before Agincourt, he has met the disguised king and told him that he would kiss his dirty shoe. During the battle, a French soldier surrenders to him, thinking him a gentleman of quality. He hears of his wife's death—he calls her Doll which is probably a mistake for Nell—and decides to turn bawd and cutpurse. *Henry V*

PLANTAGENET, LADY MARGARET: Clarence's young daughter, who, with her brother Edward Plantagenet, Earl of Warwick, hears of her father's death from the Duchess of York. Later, Richard announces that he has 'meanly matched' her in marriage and imprisoned Edward. *Richard III*

PLANTAGENET, RICHARD: *see* York

PLAYERS: Players appear in the Induction to entertain the Lord. He has them perform 'The Shrew' to the drunken Christopher Sly. *The Taming of the Shrew*

A company of actors who visit the court of Elsinore. Hamlet knows them and welcomes the First Player as an old friend, then asks him to recite a speech about the fall of Troy, speaking the beginning of it himself. He arranges for the players to perform 'The Murder of Gonzago' before the

King, the story of which is very like the way his father was murdered. He wants to test the King's reactions to the play and says he will insert some lines into it. The First Player agrees to do this. Before the performance, Hamlet gives his famous advice to the players as to how to act. Then the players perform the play, which convinces Hamlet of Claudius's guilt. *Hamlet*

POET: He breaks in on the quarrelling Brutus and Cassius in their tent and inflicts his bad rhymes on them. Brutus is furious, Cassius tolerant, but Brutus wins and the poet disappears hastily. *Julius Caesar*

He is patronized by Timon. After Timon's downfall the Poet, hearing he has gold, goes to his cave, but is driven away. *Timon of Athens*

POINS: A friend of Prince Hal who is addicted to practical jokes. In Part 1 it is Ned Poins who suggests that he and Hal disguise themselves in order to rob the robbers: Falstaff and his cronies. They do this and relieve them of their loot. He later helps tease the well-meaning Francis the drawer and also joins in the mocking of Falstaff over the robbery. In Part 2, he suggests to the Prince that they 'put on leathern jerkins and aprons' and wait upon Falstaff as drawers to see him 'in his true colours'. They do so, after which Poins disappears from the play. *1 and 2 Henry IV*

POLIXENES: The King of Bohemia and friend of King Leontes of Sicilia until the latter wrongly accuses him of being the lover of Leontes's wife, Hermione. After Camillo warns him that he has been ordered to poison him, the two men flee.
Sixteen years later we meet the wronged man again, but now he is the heavy father, anxious to prevent his son, Florizel, marrying Perdita, a shepherd girl, whom he does not know is the abandoned daughter of Leontes. Polixenes and Camillo visit the shepherd's cottage and Polixenes admits she is 'the prettiest low-born lass'. But he threatens to disinherit Florizel and kill Perdita, which forces the

135

lovers to flee to Sicilia. Polixenes follows them. All ends happily when everyone finds out the truth, and Polixenes is reconciled with Florizel, Perdita and Leontes. *The Winter's Tale*

POLONIUS: The father of Ophelia and Laertes and the Lord Chamberlain of Claudius. His advice to his son on returning to school is famous and practical, but soon he becomes a target for Hamlet's needling humour, and rather a figure of fun. He believes that Hamlet's feigned madness is due to his love for Ophelia and arranges a meeting between them during which he and Claudius listen in on their conversation: he is rather fond of spying, for he has sent his servant Reynaldo to Paris to spy on his son. Finally, this habit leads to his death. He hides himself behind the arras when Hamlet visits his mother's closet, with her permission, but when he thinks the Prince is about to attack his mother, he shouts for help and Hamlet stabs him through the curtain behind which he is hiding. 'Thou wretched, rash, intruding fool, farewell,' is Hamlet's epitaph. *Hamlet*

POLYDORE: Belarius gives Guiderius this name after kidnapping him as a child. *Cymbeline*

POMPEY: The son of Pompey the Great. He is carrying on his father's fight against Rome, but he signs a treaty with Antony, Octavius Caesar and Lepidus at Misenum and later entertains them on his galley. Mecaenas suggests killing all three, but Pompey tells him he should have done it on his own initiative; now it would be dishonourable. Later, we hear the fight has restarted and Pompey has been defeated. *Antony and Cleopatra*

POMPEY BUM: A clown who serves Mistress Overdone as a tapster and bawd. Angelo orders all the brothels to be closed, but Pompey is not prepared to give up his job and finds himself in prison. The Provost decides to pardon him if he will become the assistant executioner to Abhorson. In the prison, Pompey finds many of his old customers, which makes him feel at home. *Measure for Measure*

PORTER: He lets Macduff and Lennox into Macbeth's castle after indulging in a famous drunken soliloquy about their continual knocking at the gate. *Macbeth*

PORTIA: Brutus's wife. This 'true and honourable wife', as he calls her, begs him to confide what is on his mind to her. He promises that he will in due time. Before Caesar's assassination, she sends Lucius to the Senate to see how Brutus looks. Brutus later hears that her grief at his absence has led to her suicide by swallowing burning coals. *Julius Caesar*

A rich heiress and a heroine who is well endowed with charm and brains. By her father's will she has to marry the suitor who guesses in which of three caskets is her portrait, a gold, silver or lead one. She hopes for Bassanio who has borrowed money from Shylock to woo her, with Antonio acting as pledge for the loan. The Prince of Arragon and the Prince of Morocco are two of many who fail the casket test, but Bassanio, not being deceived by outward appearances, chooses the lead one, rightly, and wins her. She gives him a ring which he swears will never leave his finger while he lives. Gratiano and Nerissa, her gentlewoman, are also in love.

News is brought that Antonio is ruined, that he cannot repay the loan to Shylock and the Jew is demanding an agreed pound of his flesh. The men go to him as soon as they are married, while Portia decides to dress up as a man and sets out for Venice with Nerissa also in male attire. She sends to her cousin, Doctor Belario, for lawyer's clothes.

She enters the court of justice as Antonio's unknown defence counsel, with Nerissa as her clerk. She asks Shylock to show mercy, despite the justice of his case and when the amazed Shylock refuses, praising the 'wise and upright' young judge, he prepares to take the flesh. Portia then reminds him that he must not take more than a pound, or shed 'one drop of Christian blood' or all his possessions are forfeit, along with his life. Shylock is beaten and Antonio and Bassanio thank the brilliant young lawyer, who asks no reward except the ring from Bassanio's finger and Gratiano's for his clerk. Much teasing occurs back at Belmont because of this, but all is forgiven. *The Merchant of Venice*

POSTHUMUS LEONATUS: A 'poor but worthy gentleman' married to the King's daughter, Imogen. For this he is banished and goes to Italy, where the crafty Iachimo wagers that his wife is unfaithful, and that he will prove it. She is not, but he brings back enough false evidence from Britain to make Posthumus believe she is, and he orders his servant Pisanio, by letter, to kill her. He does not obey, but Posthumus later returns to Britain, thinks her dead and feels remorse. He has returned to fight for the Romans, but finds he cannot fight his fellow-countrymen. Disguised as a peasant, he joins them, only to be taken as a Roman and put in prison. He later learns that Imogen was innocent and, in despair when, disguised as the boy, Fidele, she tries to cheer him up, knocks her to the ground. When he learns the truth from his forgiving wife, he, too, shows forgiveness by sparing the now-conscience-stricken Iachimo. *Cymbeline*

PRIAM: King of Troy and father of Troilus. He is little more than a figurehead. When Troilus and Hector argue whether or not to continue fighting, he takes no real part in the discussion. Later, he cannot stop Hector from going out to fight Achilles. *Troilus and Cressida*

PRIEST: He appears in Ophelia's funeral procession and tells Laertes that because her death was 'doubtful', the ceremony is on a small scale. If he had not been commanded otherwise, she would not even have been buried in consecrated ground. *Hamlet*

PROCULEIUS: A friend of Octavius Caesar. He is sent to capture Cleopatra in her Monument and to tell her that she will not be humiliated by him. He takes her, but hands her over to Dolabella. *Antony and Cleopatra*

PROLOGUE: *see* Chorus

PROSPERO: The Duke of Milan, expelled earlier by his brother, Antonio, who took advantage of his being absorbed in books and magic. Put in a rotten boat with his daughter, Miranda, he has reached an island, where he makes the half-human Caliban and the spirit, Ariel, his servants.

When the play begins, he causes a shipwreck which strands Alonso, King of Naples, and his followers on the island, as well as his usurping brother, Antonio. Alonso's son, Ferdinand, is separated from the rest and thinks them dead. He meets Miranda and they fall in love. Prospero puts him to work as a slave to test him. Plots are afoot to kill Prospero, but the magic he wields is too strong. He releases Ferdinand from the spell which enslaved him, unites the two lovers, and has Ariel arrange a masque for them. By now he has imprisoned his enemies in a grove of lime trees where Ariel tells him they are penitent. Finding a mere spirit has more feeling than he has, his desire for vengeance goes. He forgives Antonio, reunites Ferdinand with his father, has Ariel make the sunken ship seaworthy again, releases Caliban and his friends, and prepares to sail for home as Duke. He frees Ariel as his last magical act.

Prospero has some magnificent poetry to speak, but some find him too much of an all-powerful, all-knowing headmaster. He certainly becomes more human when he finds that his daughter has grown up and truly loves Ferdinand, but his nobility shows at the end when he forgives his enemies. *The Tempest*

PROTEUS: A gentleman of Verona, and not very attractive as a friend or a lover. His friend Valentine goes to Milan, while he stays at home to be near Julia. Then his father sends him to Milan. There he falls in love with Valentine's Silvia and has him banished by telling the Duke, her father, that Valentine means to elope with her.

Meanwhile, Julia comes to Milan disguised as a boy, 'Sebastian' and watches Proteus making love—without success—to Silvia, who escapes to find Valentine. He goes after her with Julia and the cowardly Thurio whom the

Duke wishes his daughter to marry. Silvia is captured by outlaws and rescued by Proteus who is about to take her by force when Valentine, now the captain of the outlaws, arrives to rescue her. Ashamed of himself, Proteus asks Valentine to forgive him, which he does, then he finds out who Sebastian is and she forgives him too. He claims that inconstancy is man's one fault and decides that Julia is attractive, too. *The Two Gentlemen of Verona*

PROVOST: The kindly governor of a jail in Vienna. He tries to stop the Deputy, Angelo, from condemning Claudio to be executed and watches Isabella pleading for her brother's life. He also pardons Pompey the Bawd as long as he will agree to become the assistant to the executioner. The disguised Duke persuades him to execute Barnardine instead of Claudio, but the Provost manages to send the head of a pirate to Angelo instead. At the end, the Duke praises him and promises him a better position. *Measure for Measure*

PUBLIUS: A senator who escorts Caesar to the Senate on the day of his assassination. Brutus tells the shaken old man after the killing that no harm is intended him, and Cassius advises him to flee in case the crowds trample him. *Julius Caesar*

Titus's nephew and son of Marcus Andronicus. He is kind to Titus when he is apparently mad and later assists at the execution of Chiron and Demetrius. *Titus Andronicus*

PUCK: A mischievous spirit who serves Oberon, also called Robin Goodfellow. Oberon, having quarrelled with his wife, Titania, makes Puck bring a juice which will make her fall in love with whatever she sees when she wakes. When he has brought it, Oberon orders him to put some juice on the eyelids of Demetrius. He puts it on Lysander instead of Demetrius which results in a series of emotional mix-ups between the four young Athenians who have fled to the forest.

Meanwhile, Puck has turned Bottom the Weaver's head into an ass's head, so that Titania on waking falls in love with him, much to Oberon's pleasure. Oberon proceeds to put right the muddle that Puck's mistakes have caused, ordering him to lead the men astray in the forest. Puck later removes Bottom's ass head. He ends the play hoping that 'we shadows' have not offended. *A Midsummer Night's Dream*

Q

QUEEN: Cymbeline's evil second wife who hates him and plans to put Cloten, her lumpish son from another marriage, on the throne. Having failed to wed him to Cymbeline's daughter Imogen, she plans to poison both of them. Failing in this too, she goes mad with despair and her deathbed repentance is later reported. *Cymbeline*

Richard's wife. She overhears a gardener telling a servant about her husband's deposition and later, outside the Tower, accuses him of weakness but bids him a sorrowful farewell. *Richard II*

QUICKLY, MISTRESS: The hostess of the Boar's Head Tavern, Eastcheap. In Part 1, she has a husband, though we do not meet him. Falstaff alleges that her inn is 'turned bawdy house; they pick pockets'. Be that as it may, he owes her money, as we learn in her second scene when she appeals to Prince Hal. In Part 2, she is a widow and claims that Falstaff has said he will marry her. She tries to have him arrested for debt, but relents. Falstaff visits her and Doll Tearsheet before going to Gloucestershire. At the end she and Doll are arrested for helping Pistol beat a man to death. *1 and 2 Henry IV*

She becomes Doctor Caius's housekeeper and a busy go-between, not caring which of Anne Page's suitors she helps. She also gets used by the merry wives to carry messages to Falstaff. Pistol, admiring the way she attracts money, decides to marry her. In the Windsor Forest scene she plays the Fairy Queen in the baiting of Falstaff. *The Merry Wives of Windsor*

As Nell Quickly, she and Pistol are married. She describes Falstaff's death in one of the greatest speeches in Shakespeare, then says goodbye to Pistol, Nym and the Boy who are off to the wars. Pistol later learns she is dead. Confusingly, he calls her Doll on this occasion, which is probably a mistake for Nell. *Henry V*

QUINCE, PETER: A carpenter and the director of 'Pyramus and Thisbe', running the rehearsals, when Bottom does not interfere, and speaking the Prologue. According to Hippolyta, he speaks it 'like a child on a recorder; a sound, but not in government'. *A Midsummer Night's Dream*

QUINTUS: One of Titus's sons. He and his brother, Martius, fall in a pit into which the sons of Tamora have hurled the murdered Bassianus. Quintus and Martius are accused of the murder and executed. *Titus Andronicus*

R

RAGOZINE: The dead murderer whose head is substituted for Claudio's and sent to Angelo. *Measure for Measure*

RAMBURES, LORD: One of the French lords who deride the English before Agincourt, where he is killed. *Henry V*

RATCLIFF, SIR RICHARD: He leads Rivers, Grey and Vaughan to their executions at Pomfret, and later, with Lovel, takes Hastings to the block and returns with his head. He is with Richard at Bosworth, entering his tent after the ghosts' scene to tell him it is time to arm. 'Be not afraid of shadows,' he tells the King. He is killed in the battle. *Richard III*

REGAN: Lear's second daughter and, in A. C. Bradley's opinion, 'the most hideous human being in Shakespeare'. She is Cornwall's wife. In the opening scene, when Lear divides up his kingdom, she vies with her sister, Goneril, in claims of how much she loves her father, while the loving Cordelia stays silent and is disinherited. Soon she is demanding that Lear dismiss his followers, and she and Cornwall tell Gloucester to bar his doors to Lear. Because Gloucester wants to help Lear, Cornwall gouges out his eye with Regan urging him on, then, when Cornwall is wounded by a servant, kills the servant while Cornwall gouges out the other eye. Cornwall dies and Regan becomes Edmund's lover. Goneril wants Edmund too, and the sisters argue over him. Goneril poisons Regan, then kills herself. Those who champion Regan's claim to be the more appalling cite the pettiness of her personality; the ghastly Goneril at least possesses a certain savage grandeur. *King Lear*

REIGNIER, DUKE OF ANJOU: He supports the Dauphin and Joan of Arc. He is father of Margaret, who is captured by Suffolk and, with Reignier's permission, marries Henry. Her father's main concern is that he can 'quietly enjoy mine own, the county Maine and Anjou'. *1 Henry VI*

REYNALDO: A servant of Polonius sent by him to spy on his son, Laertes, back at school in Paris. *Hamlet*

RICHARD II: The flawed hero of the play of that name, his intelligent sensitive nature being offset by self-indulgence, incompetence and a genius for self-dramatization. As Richard's fortunes decline, however, he grows in stature. The play begins with John of Gaunt's son, Bolingbroke, accusing Mowbray of embezzling funds and murdering Gloucester. Richard orders a trial by combat, but, instead, banishes Mowbray for life and Bolingbroke for ten years. When Gaunt dies, Richard confiscates his estate to pay for an Irish war, and Bolingbroke comes back to claim his rights. The King returns from Ireland to find himself deserted by nearly everyone and flees to Flint Castle. Bolingbroke appears and demands his rights, promising to lay down his 'glittering arms' if he can get them. Richard agrees, but knows his power is waning. He is taken to London where Bolingbroke summons him and takes his crown. Northumberland taunts him with a list of crimes he will not read. He calls for a glass, looks at his face and smashes the glass on the ground.

He is led to the Tower, passing the Queen on the way, who tells him he has been too weak, but sadly bids him farewell. Then he is taken to Pomfret where, after mournfully soliloquizing on his fate, he is murdered.

Richard's flair for language never deserts him, nor does his power of exaggeration. He claims his situation is worse than Christ's after Judas betrayed Him. He is an egoist, a weak man, safe, as he thinks, in the divine right of kings, and has entrusted England to favourites. Yet he grows in nobility and sheer courage: in the end he kills two of his murderers before he dies. His patriotism is never in doubt. When he lands in Wales he salutes the earth with his hand, 'though rebels wound thee with their horses' hoofs'. *Richard II*

RICHARD III (GLOUCESTER): We first meet Shakespeare's Demon King, Richard Plantagenet, when he kills Somerset at the Battle of St. Albans (unhistorically: he was aged 8). *2 Henry VI*. He is made Duke of Gloucester by his brother, Edward IV, and rapidly develops into the villain we love to hate, though the power struggles portrayed in this play make him only the most spectacular amongst many until he reveals the depths of his villainy. At first he supports his father, York, and Edward loyally, though in a great soliloquy he shows he wants the crown and how he resents his crooked back and shrivelled arm, and says he will 'set the murderous Machiavel to school'. At Tewkesbury he helps kill Edward, Prince of Wales, then hastens to the Tower to make, as his brother Clarence, says, 'a bloody supper' out of Henry VI, whom he murders. In another fine speech he sets the scene for the ambitious super-villain. *3 Henry VI* His own play opens with the incomparable 'Now is the winter of our discontent' speech. He then sets out to remove all obstacles between him and the crown. He has Clarence murdered, woos Lady Anne who hates him for killing her husband at Tewkesbury, and seems to hypnotize her to win her in an electric scene. Edward dies and Richard executes the Queen's brother, Rivers, and her son, Grey, also Hastings, and places Edward, Prince of Wales, and his brother in the Tower. With his leading crony, Buckingham, he arranges for the citizens of London to acclaim him king, then has the princes killed and helps Anne to the grave. Buckingham finally rebels against him but is caught and executed, and Richard himself meets his end at Bosworth, killed by Richmond, later Henry VII. Whether the historic Richard was better or worse than his contemporaries will probably never be known now. What matters dramatically is that the play's Tudor version of history, plus the young Shakespeare's early genius in full flower, produced the most glorious, sardonic Satan rampant in drama, utterly courageous, utterly amoral and very entertaining. 'There is no creature loves me,' he laments before Bosworth. Millions of playgoers down the centuries would dispute him. *Richard III*

RICHMOND (HENRY VII): He appears briefly as a 'pretty lad' who Henry says 'will prove our country's bliss'. *3 Henry VI*. He becomes an idealized hero, very different from the real Henry. He appears in the last act to defeat Richard at Bosworth, after having been comforted by the ghosts of Richard's victims the previous night. *Richard III*

RIVERS: Lord Rivers, brother of Elizabeth, Edward IV's Queen, is told by her that Warwick has been captured by the King. *3 Henry VI*. He is led to his execution at Pomfret, after remembering Richard II's death there and Margaret's anti-Yorkist curses. *Richard III*

RINALDO: The Countess's steward. He tells her that Helena loves Bertram. Later, he reads the Countess a farewell letter from Helena. *All's Well that Ends Well*

ROBIN: *see* Boy

ROBIN GOODFELLOW: *see* Puck

RODERIGO: A Venetian gentleman in love with Desdemona. He falls into the clutches of Iago, who pretends to help him. In Cyprus, Iago involves Roderigo in a fight with Cassio which leads to Cassio's disgrace, and later tells him he must murder Cassio, his alleged rival in love. Roderigo bungles the job and Iago murders him to stop him betraying his plot. *Othello*

ROGERO: He is the Second Gentleman who reports to his friends that Perdita is found and that Paulina keeps going to the house where Hermione's statue (actually Hermione) is kept. *The Winter's Tale*

ROMEO: The play's tragic young hero. He is the son of Montague whose clan is feuding with the Capulets. He hopelessly and rather self-indulgently loves Rosaline until he meets Juliet, Capulet's daughter, at a masked ball in her house and they fall in love. Then they find out each other's identity. Romeo has his famous love scene with Juliet, and the next day is secretly married to her by Friar Laurence. Juliet's cousin, Tybalt, meets Romeo and his friends, Mercutio and Benvolio, in the street and tries to pick a quarrel with him. He refuses to fight until Mercutio takes on Tybalt and is killed. Then Romeo kills Tybalt and flees. The Prince banishes him.

In despair, Romeo goes to Friar Laurence who stops him killing himself. He calms him and sends him to Juliet. After they have spent the night together he escapes to Mantua where he hears she is dead, though actually the Friar has given her a potion to make her seem dead. He goes to her tomb, kills Paris who hoped to marry her, then poisons himself to die at her side.

Romeo grows in stature through the play, from a love-sick boy who is rightly mocked by Mercutio to a truly tragic figure. Enthusiastic, idealistic and rash, his impetuous nature and a cruel fate lead him to disaster. His verse is early Shakespeare at its finest, and his magnificent death speech is an affirmation of love without any self-pity. No actor has made his name, however, in this difficult part, which, until Mercutio's death, is overshadowed by that glamorous Renaissance Man. *Romeo and Juliet*

ROSALIND: The daughter of the banished Duke and the play's delightful and witty heroine. She is still at Court as the companion of Celia, daughter of the usurping Duke. She falls in love with Orlando, but is banished and goes to the Forest of Arden with Celia and the jester, Touchstone, having disguised herself as a youth, Ganymede.

In Arden she meets Orlando again, who has also been forced to flee. He has decorated trees with poems to her and, after teasing him, she says she will cure him of love if she pretends to be Rosalind and he woos her. She meets the scornful Phebe and criticizes her for rejecting her lover, Silvius. Phebe promptly falls for her. Finally, she reveals who she is and is reunited with her father and marries Orlando. All ends happily and she speaks the epilogue. A most attractive heroine, her witty chatter cannot conceal her tender and loving nature. *As You Like It*

ROSALINE: The witty lady-in-waiting of the Princess of France. They and two other ladies meet the King of Navarre and three courtiers who have all forsworn women for three years. All fall in love, Berowne with Rosaline. Their verbal duels anticipate those of Beatrice and Benedick, and finally Rosaline triumphs when the cynical Berowne confesses he loves her. At the end, when the ladies go home, she says she will marry him in a year if, in the meantime, he visits the sick and makes them smile. Berowne says she is a whitely wanton with 'two pitch black balls stuck in her face for eyes'. *Love's Labour's Lost*

Romeo's love before he meets Juliet. She does not appear, unless, perhaps, at the Capulet's ball. *Romeo and Juliet*

ROSENCRANTZ: *see* Guildenstern

ROSS: A Scottish nobleman. He tells Duncan that Macbeth has defeated the rebels and the Norwegians, then tells Macbeth he has been made Thane of Cawdor. He is at Glamis when Duncan is murdered and later explains to Lady Macduff why her husband has had to flee to England. He breaks the news to Macduff that she and his children have been murdered and returns to Scotland with Malcolm. *Macbeth*

ROSS, LORD: He joins Bolingbroke when the latter's lands are confiscated by the King. *Richard II*

ROTHERAM, THOMAS: Archbishop of York. He resigns his seal of office to Queen Elizabeth when he hears that Richard has executed her brother, Rivers, and her son, Grey, and offers to take her to sanctuary. *Richard III*

ROUSILLON, COUNTESS OF: A kindly woman, the mother of the appalling Bertram, and Helena's guardian. She treats her as a daughter and encourages her to marry Bertram. She is furious at his treatment of her and tries to bring the two together again when Bertram abandons her rather than live with her. Shaw called her Shakespeare's most beautiful old woman. *All's Well that Ends Well*

RUGBY, JOHN: Dr. Caius's servant. Mistress Quickly, the housekeeper, says he is honest, willing and kind, his worst fault being that he is 'given to prayer; he is something peevish that way'. Caius tries to make this simple man use his rapier on Sir Hugh Evans, but he cannot fence. *The Merry Wives of Windsor*

RUMOUR: He (or she) brings false news to the 'crafty-sick' Northumberland that his son, Hotspur, has won at Shrewsbury. *2 Henry IV*

RUTLAND, EARL OF: York's youngest son, murdered by Clifford at Wakefield after York has killed Clifford's father. *3 Henry VI*

S

SALARINO AND SALANIO AND SALERIO: The first two are friends of Antonio and Bassanio. They try to cheer Antonio in the first scene, and Salarino helps Lorenzo elope with Shylock's daughter, Jessica. Both men have a scene with a furious Shylock after her flight, and discuss Antonio's situation. Later, Salarino commiserates with Antonio on his way to jail. Salerio may, confusingly, be a misprint for Salarino; he does not appear in some editions of the play. Assuming he does exist, he comes to Portia's house to say that Antonio's ships are lost, and he is at Antonio's trial. *The Merchant of Venice*

SALISBURY, EARL OF: He fights at Agincourt. *Henry V*. He is killed by a cannon ball when observing Orleans. *1 Henry VI*

A Yorkist. He is a friend of Gloucester and an enemy of Suffolk, whom he demands be banished after the murder of Gloucester. He is also an enemy of Cardinal Beaufort and sees him die. He joins York to fight at St. Albans like a 'winter lion', says York, and young Richard Crookback is much impressed by the old man's valour. *2 Henry VI*

He suspects that John has had Arthur killed and dislikes his policies. With other lords, he goes over to Lewis the Dauphin, but when he hears that he and his companions are to be murdered by Lewis once he has succeeded in his invasion plans, he returns to John's side. He is present when the King dies and declares himself a supporter of Henry III. *King John*

He is loyal to the King. He tries to stop Richard's Welshmen dispersing and later conspires against Henry and is captured and executed. *Richard II*

SAMPSON: One of Capulet's servants. Meeting Abraham and Balthasar, both Montagues, he bites his thumb at them, which begins the street fight at the start of the play. *Romeo and Juliet*

SATURNINUS: He becomes Emperor when his father dies and Titus declines to be elected. He promises to marry Titus's daughter, Lavinia, but when his brother, Bassianus, carries her off, he marries Tamora, the evil Queen of the Goths. He has two of Titus's sons executed who are wrongly thought to have killed Bassianus. When Titus finds that the culprits, who also raped and mutilated Lavinia, are Tamora's sons, he serves them to Tamora baked in a pie, then he kills Lavinia to end her shame. Saturninus kills Titus and Titus's son, Lucius, kills Saturninus. *Titus Andronicus*

SAY, LORD: The Lord Treasurer. He is captured by Jack Cade and accused of everything from the loss of Normandy to erecting a grammar school. He defends himself well, but is rushed to his death, and his head is brought in on a pole. *2 Henry VI*

SCALES, LORD: He is reported captured by the French. *1 Henry VI*. He is Governor of the Tower when Cade's rebels attack London. *2 Henry VI*

SCARUS: A friend of Antony. He fights bravely for him, is wounded and rewarded with golden armour by Cleopatra. He later describes Cleopatra's fleet to Antony: 'Swallows have built In Cleopatra's sails their nests.' *Antony and Cleopatra*

SCROOP, LORD (SCROPE): The son of Sir Stephen Scroop, he has plotted with Cambridge and Grey to kill the King as he sets out for France. The plot is discovered and Henry has them executed. *Henry V*

SCROOP (SCROPE), RICHARD: The Archbishop of York and a brother of Sir Stephen. In Part 1, he supports Hotspur's rebellion, but is not at Shrewsbury for the battle. In Part 2, he is persuaded by Prince John of Lancaster to dismiss his men and then is treacherously arrested and executed. *1 and 2 Henry IV*

SCROOP, SIR STEPHEN: A loyal follower of the King who tells him that Bushy, Green and Wiltshire, Scroop's brother, have been executed by Bolingbroke. *Richard II*

SEA-CAPTAIN: A pirate who captures Suffolk's ship. Blaming the earl for many of England's woes, he has him killed. *2 Henry VI*

Captain of a ship carrying Viola and Sebastian which is wrecked on the coast of Illyria. He tells Viola that her brother may be alive and that he will present her to Duke Orsino as a eunuch. *Twelfth Night*

SEACOLE (SEACOAL), GEORGE: The Second Watchman who arrests Borachio and Conrade. His brother, FRANCIS, called a scribe by Dogberry, acts as Sexton (clerk) at the trial. *Much Ado About Nothing*

SEBASTIAN: Viola's twin brother. He thinks his sister is drowned, as he tells his friend, Antonio. While looking around Illyria, where he has been shipwrecked, he is mistaken for Cesario (Viola disguised as a boy) and forced to fight a duel with Sir Andrew. He wounds the foolish knight, then Olivia mistakes him for her beloved Cesario and rushes him, astonished but pleased, to the altar. All is explained when he is reunited with Viola. *Twelfth Night*

SELEUCUS: The Queen's treasurer. He tells Caesar when she gives an account of her wealth, that she has only revealed half of it in the inventory. *Antony and Cleopatra.*

SEMPRONIUS: One of the flattering lords who refuse to lend Timon money when he loses his fortune. Sempronius claims to be offended at being asked last. *Timon of Athens*

SERGEANT: A badly wounded soldier who reports Macbeth's victory over the rebels and Norwegians to King Duncan. *Macbeth*

SERVANT OF THE LORD CHIEF JUSTICE: He sees Falstaff and is told to fetch him; Falstaff pretends to be deaf and abuses him. *2 Henry IV*

SERVILIUS: One of Timon's servants. He tries to get a loan from Lucius for his master, but fails. *Timon of Athens*

SEYTON: One of Macbeth's officers. He reports to him about the English advance and later tells him that Lady Macbeth is dead. *Macbeth*

SHADOW, SIMON: One of those conscripted by Shallow to serve with Falstaff. *2 Henry IV*

SHALLOW, ROBERT: A country justice in the Cotswolds. He recruits some men to serve with Falstaff, whom he knew years before when he was at Clement's Inn. He boasts a lot about his wild youth, though Falstaff, when he is gone, says how prone 'we old men are to this vice of lying'. He admits though that the old man, who looked like a forked radish when he was young—and naked—was as lecherous as a monkey. Their reminiscences have great charm: 'We have heard the chimes at midnight, Master Shallow,' Falstaff says to him.
Falstaff returns from the wars via Gloucestershire and Shallow lends him a thousand pounds. They race to London at the news that Prince Hal is King, and Shallow sees Hal's rejection. 'Master Shallow, I owe you a thousand pounds,' says Falstaff with dignity after it and promises to pay the debt, but both are rushed to the Fleet prison. *2 Henry IV*

Shallow is now very old, still a justice, and is Slender's cousin. In peppery mood he complains that Falstaff has beaten ten of his men, killed his deer and broken open his lodge, and he wants to make a Star-Chamber matter of it. He does his best to win Anne Page for his stupid cousin,

Slender, whom Page favours, but has to do the wooing for Slender, without success. *The Merry Wives of Windsor*

SHEPHERD, OLD: Joan of Arc's father. He bemoans her impending death until she insolently abuses him and denies her parentage, claiming to be born of royal stock. Furiously, he says hanging is too good for her and wants her burnt. *1 Henry VI*

The reputed father of Perdita, the abandoned daughter of Leontes and Hermione. The kindly old man has found her and brought her up as his daughter from infancy. She falls in love with Florizel, the son of Polixenes, who condemns him to death for daring to allow the match. The three escape to Sicilia with the Shepherd's son (*see* Clown). There, father and son are both made 'gentlemen born'. *The Winter's Tale*

SHYLOCK: A rich Jewish moneylender and the play's great artistic creation. He lends Antonio 3,000 ducats for three months, after which he will claim a pound of the merchant's flesh. Shylock hates him because he has often been spurned like a dog by him. While he is dining with Bassanio, Shylock's daughter, Jessica, elopes with Lorenzo, taking much of his fortune with her: he bitterly resents the loss of both.

Meanwhile, Antonio's ships are reported wrecked and Shylock demands his bond. 'I will have the heart of him,' he says. In court Shylock states his case, but Portia appears, disguised as a lawyer: her husband, Bassanio, has un-wittingly caused the whole affair by borrowing from Antonio to go wooing her. At first Shylock admires the lawyer, but Portia confounds him by saying that his life and property will be forfeit if he takes more than a pound of flesh or sheds a drop of Antonio's blood, and that his life will be forfeit anyway for his plan. The Duke pardons him and gives him back half his money if, as Antonio requests, he bequeathes it to Lorenzo and turns Christian. In contrast to Marlowe's 'Jew of Malta', Shakespeare's Jew is a human being. His most famous speech, 'Hath not a

Jew eyes?' is typical of Shakespeare's humanity, and many of Shylock's opponents are fortune-hunters or idlers. Shylock was a villain to the Elizabethan and a villain he remains, though it is his daughter's defection and the insults to his race and faith that turn him implacable. *The Merchant of Venice*

SICINIUS VELUTUS: *see* Brutus, Junius

SILENCE: A Gloucestershire justice and the cousin of Shallow. He is not totally silent in his first scene with him and then Falstaff, but his moment comes when Falstaff returns from the wars. Silence gets drunk, sings heartily and is carried to bed. Falstaff had no idea he was 'a man of this mettle' but Silence confesses to have been 'merry twice and once ere now'. *2 Henry IV*

SILIUS: One of Ventidius's officers. He vainly urges Ventidius to pursue the retreating Parthians. *Antony and Cleopatra*

SILVIA: The Duke of Milan's beautiful daughter, who loves and is loved by Valentine. Her father wants her to marry the cowardly Thurio. Valentine's alleged friend, Proteus, wants her and does his best to break up her romance with Valentine by telling her father they are going to elope. Proteus also tries to make love to her himself, and later, when she has fled to find Valentine, is about to rape her when Valentine appears. All ends happily. She inspires the song, 'Who is Silvia?' *The Two Gentlemen of Verona*

SILVIUS: A shepherd in love with the scornful Phebe, even having to carry a love letter from her to Ganymede (actually Rosalind, disguised as a boy). Rosalind has her doubts about him for being so feeble, but when she reveals herself, his adored Phebe agrees rather surprisingly to marry him for his devotion. *As You Like It*

SIMONIDES: King of Pentapolis and father of Thaisa. He allows the ill-dressed stranger, Pericles, to marry her after winning her in a tournament, though he pretends for a time that he has bewitched her. A kindly man and a good ruler. *Pericles*

SIMPCOX, SAUNDER: He and his wife are impostors who tell the King that Simpcox's sight has been cured by a miracle at St. Albans. Gloucester is not taken in, proves him a fraud, then cures his alleged lameness by having him whipped, at which he runs away. The onlookers shout: 'A miracle!' *2 Henry VI*

SIMPLE: Slender's servant. His stupid master hopes to marry Anne Page, and Simple is sent to Mistress Quickly with a letter from Evans asking her to help in the wooing. Simple hides in a closet when Dr. Caius appears. The doctor finds him and he is sent packing with a challenge to Evans. Later, he gets teased by Falstaff and the Host of the Garter Inn. *The Merry Wives of Windsor*

SIWARD: The Earl of Northumberland who leads 10,000 men sent by Edward the Confessor to help Malcolm overthrow Macbeth. His son, YOUNG SIWARD, is killed by Macbeth. *Macbeth*

SLENDER: Shallow's half-witted cousin. It is Shallow who suggests he woos Anne Page. Not much of a ladies' man, or any sort of man, he has to have Shallow and Sir Hugh Evans do his wooing for him; in fact, he tells Anne that for his part he would have little or nothing to do with her. However, Master Page approves of him and arranges for him to elope with Anne during the baiting of Falstaff in Windsor Forest. Anne instead elopes with Fenton and Slender runs away with a fairy dressed in white who turns out to be a postmaster's 'great lubberly boy'. *The Merry Wives of Windsor*

SLY, CHRISTOPHER: In the Induction, the drunken tinker who finds himself taken by a Lord to his chamber and dressed up. When he wakes up he finds himself with a 'wife' who tells him he has recovered from fifteen years as a lunatic. To stop him relapsing, a performance is laid on for him. *The Taming of the Shrew*

SMITH: A weaver and one of Cade's rebels. He does not think much of Cade's claim to be Mortimer, but accuses the Clerk of Chatham of reading and writing, for which the Clerk is hanged. *2 Henry VI*

SNARE: A sheriff's officer sent with Fang to arrest Falstaff. *2 Henry IV*

SNOUT, TOM: An Athenian tinker cast by Quince as Pyramus's father in 'Pyramus and Thisbe'. Finally, he plays the Wall, speaking his speech so memorably that Demetrius comments: 'It is the wittiest partition that I ever heard discourse.' *A Midsummer Night's Dream*

SNUG: An Athenian joiner. He is, he confesses, slow of study, so volunteers to play the lion in 'Pyramus and Thisbe'. Bottom says he must announce who he really is so that the ladies will not be frightened, and this he does. He roars very well and is congratulated by Demetrius. *A Midsummer Night's Dream*

SOLINUS: The Duke of Ephesus. His city is the enemy of Syracuse, and when Aegeon of Syracuse lands at Ephesus, he condemns him to death, granting him a pardon if he can raise a ransom of 1,000 marks in a day. When the mistaken identities are sorted out, he pardons Aegeon. *The Comedy of Errors*

SOMERSET: *see* Beaufort

SOMERVILLE, SIR JOHN: A Lancastrian, who tells Warwick that Clarence and his army are near. *3 Henry VI*

SON WHO HAS KILLED HIS FATHER: He kills a man in battle and finds it is his own father. *3 Henry VI*

SOOTHSAYERS: There are three in Shakespeare. One tells Caesar to beware the Ides of March and, on the day of his death, when Caesar says the Ides have come, replies 'Ay Caesar; but not gone.' *Julius Caesar*. The Soothsayer tells

Cleopatra's women, Charmian and Iras, that they will out-live her and tells Antony that Caesar's fortunes will rise higher than his. *Antony and Cleopatra*. The Soothsayer tells Lucius that the Romans will win the battle and later explains a label that Posthumus has found on his bosom after his vision. *Cymbeline*

SOUTHWELL, JOHN: A priest and one of those who conjure up a spirit for the Duchess of Gloucester. He is caught and condemned to be hanged. *2 Henry VI*

SPEED: Valentine's clownish, but bright, servant who goes with him to Milan. He is captured by outlaws with him and, when the outlaws want to make Valentine their king, advises him to accept. He has several scenes with Proteus's servant, Launce. *The Two Gentlemen of Verona*

STAFFORD, SIR HUMPHREY AND WILLIAM STAFFORD: They lead troops to try to stop the rebel, Cade, at Blac'-heath, but are both killed. *2 Henry VI*

STAFFORD, LORD: He is ordered by Edward IV: 'Go levy men, and make prepare for war.' He is a Yorkist; the other Stafford, mentioned as being dead, is a Lancastrian. *3 Henry VI*

STANLEY, SIR JOHN: He takes the exiled Duchess of Gloucester to the Isle of Man. *2 Henry VI*

STANLEY, LORD THOMAS: He claims to be loyal to Richard, who suspects him because he is related by marriage to the Tudors. When Richmond lands in England, Stanley's son, George, is kept as a hostage by Richard. This makes Stanley warn Richmond that he cannot help him at Bosworth, but in the event, he holds his forces back before the battle begins and helps sway the balance. Richard orders his son to be beheaded, but it is not done. Henry VII made him Earl of Derby, by which title he is known—wrongly—in some editions of the play. *Richard III*

STANLEY, SIR WILLIAM: The brother of Lord Stanley who (without any lines) helps Edward IV escape from Middleham Castle. *3 Henry VI*. He is mentioned as having gone against Richard. *Richard III*

STARVELING, ROBIN: An Athenian tailor. Quince casts him as Thisbe's mother in the interlude, 'Pyramus and Thisbe'. A pacifist, he wants killing left out. Finally, he plays Moonshine, but is barracked by the audience and does not get far before he is forced to stop. *A Midsummer Night's Dream*

STEPHANO: A servant of Portia who tells Lorenzo and Jessica that she is returning to Belmont. *The Merchant of Venice*

The King of Naples' drunken butler. He sees a four-legged monster which is actually Caliban and Trinculo under a gaberdine: he had hoped to make money out of it. He gives Caliban wine, and Caliban suggests that they kill his master, Prospero, and Stephano can be king of the island. The spirit, Ariel, hears the plan and leads the three drunks into a 'filthy-mantled pool', then sets spirits disguised as dogs onto them, but not before they have stolen some clothes 'planted' on them by Ariel. At the end Prospero pardons them handsomely. *The Tempest*

STRANGERS: They tell Lucius of Timon's ruin. He is apparently appalled, but when Timon's servant, Lucilius, comes asking for money for his master, he refuses. The strangers make pointed comments when Lucius has left, about false friends and flatterers. *Timon of Athens*

STRATO: A servant of Brutus. In a moving scene after Brutus's defeat at Philippi, he holds the sword on to which his master runs, but, first, Strato asks to shake his hand. He becomes the servant of Octavius. *Julius Caesar*

SUFFOLK, DUKE OF: One of those who hate Wolsey, he delights in taunting him on his downfall. He acts as High Steward in Anne Bullen's coronation. He has been playing some game with the King in a later scene and has managed to beat him. He is the least enthusiastic of the nobles who plot unsuccessfully against Cranmer and is last seen at the christening of the infant, Elizabeth. *Henry VIII*

SUFFOLK, EARL OF: He becomes a Lancastrian, picking a red rose in the Temple Garden. He captures Margaret of Anjou, falls in love with her, but being married, arranges that she shall marry Henry and be his mistress. *1 Henry VI*. He now becomes a Duke and a power in the land. He has the Duchess of Gloucester banished for sorcery and her husband murdered. For this he is banished himself. He is captured by pirates off Kent. The pirate captain hates him for his reputation and he is murdered by a sailor named Walter Whitemore. *2 Henry VI*

SURREY, EARL OF: The King asks him and Warwick if they have read letters about the northern rebellion. *2 Henry IV*

He rejoices in Wolsey's downfall, calling him 'proud traitor' and a 'scarlet sin'. He is at Anne Bullen's Coronation. For his father, *see* Norfolk. *Henry VIII*

SURREY, DUKE OF: He defends Aumerle against an accusation that he has murdered Gloucester. Later, he joins a rebellion against Bolingbroke and is captured and executed. *Richard II*

SURVEYOR TO THE DUKE OF BUCKINGHAM: He has been dismissed by the Duke and at Buckingham's trial falsely testifies against him, claiming that he heard him say that he would put a knife into the King. *Henry VIII*

T

TAILOR: He shows Katharine a fine gown, but Petruchio, busy taming her, calls it ugly and refuses to let her wear it. *The Taming of the Shrew*

TALBOT, LORD: The daring commander of the English forces in France, first seen fighting the French, including Joan of Arc, at Orleans. On one occasion this 'fiend of hell', as the Bastard of Orleans calls him, surprises the French and forces them to flee in their shirts. The Countess of Auverne later thinks she has him as a prisoner, but he has brought along his soldiers and she feasts him instead. At Rouen, Sir John Fastolfe acts like a coward, and Talbot, who is later made Earl of Shrewsbury for his capture of the town, strips Fastolfe of his Order of the Garter after Henry's coronation in Paris. Henry orders Talbot to chastise Burgundy for changing sides. However, he is trapped with his son, JOHN TALBOT, by the French near Bordeaux. His brave son refuses to flee when his father, who has not seen him for seven years, tells him to, and they are both killed, Talbot dying with his arms about the dead youth. *1 Henry VI*

TAMORA. The vengeful Queen of the Goths. She is captured by Titus with her three sons, but marries the Roman Emperor Saturninus. Enflamed by Titus's sacrifice of one of her sons, she plots with her Moorish lover, Aaron, to get her revenge. This results in her remaining two sons, Demetrius and Chiron, raping and mutilating Titus's daughter, Lavinia, after they have murdered Bassianus, her husband. Two of Titus's sons are accused of the murder, and executed, and Aaron cuts off one of Titus's hands. His revenge is spectacular. When he finds that Tamora's sons were the guilty ones, he has them killed, baked in a pie and given to their unsuspecting mother to eat. He then kills Tamora. This 'heinous tiger' has earlier had a child by Aaron. *Titus Andronicus*

TAURUS, STATILIUS: He commands Octavius Caesar's army at Actium, being ordered not to attack on land 'until we have done at sea'. *Antony and Cleopatra*

TEARSHEET, DOLL: Falstaff's drunken mistress. A lady of lively language, she sups with him at the Boar's Head

Tavern and has a furious slanging match which nearly ends in bloodshed and a general fight. She seems genuinely upset when Falstaff has to go to the wars. She is sent to prison at the end because there have been some deaths over her. *2 Henry IV*

THAISA: King Simonides of Pentapolis' daughter. Pericles wins her in a tournament and though she knows little about him, she is determined to marry him. On the voyage home to Tyre, she apparently dies giving birth to Marina and is buried at sea. Her coffin lands at Ephesus where she is brought back to life by Cerimon. Thinking Pericles dead, she becomes a votaress at the Temple of Diana, to be reunited fourteen years later with both Pericles and Marina. *Pericles*

THALIARD: A lord of Antioch. Antiochus orders him to kill Pericles who has found out about his incestuous relationship with his daughter. He follows him to Tyre and is delighted to find that Pericles has sailed away. *Pericles*

THERSITES: A deformed, cynical, foul-mouthed, chorus-like commentator in the Greek camp, scurrilously abusing most of the main characters and allowing humans only one motive: lechery. Ajax is so incensed by his jibes that he beats him. Thersites sees Cressida betray Troilus with the Greek Diomedes. In the final fighting he is attacked by Margelon. He avoids being killed by this bastard son of Priam by pointing out he too is a bastard and that they should not 'bite one another'. Earlier his instinct for self-preservation had saved him from an even greater enemy, Hector himself. 'Art thou for Hector's match?' asks the great man. 'No,' replies Thersites, 'I am a rascal; a scurvy, railing knave; a very filthy rogue.' 'I do believe thee: live,' Hector tells him. *Troilus and Cressida*

THESEUS: The Duke of Athens. He is preparing for his wedding to Hippolyta and wants his Master of the Revels to arrange 'merriments' for him. These turn out to be the Interlude of 'Pyramus and Thisbe', performed by the

Mechanicals. He tells Hermia to obey her father, Egeus, and marry Lysander, but later, when he sees that Demetrius loves Helena, he overrules Egeus and Hermia can marry her Lysander. He invites the four lovers to enjoy a triple wedding ceremony with himself and his bride. A courteous English gentleman, he congratulates Bottom and Co. on their lamentable performance, which he says was 'very notably discharged'. *A Midsummer Night's Dream*

THISBE (THISBY): The heroine of the Interlude, 'Pyramus and Thisbe', the part being played by Francis Flute. *A Midsummer Night's Dream*

THURIO: A rich man considered a suitable match by the Duke of Milan for his daughter, Silvia, who loves Valentine. When Silvia goes to find Valentine, he follows her, but when challenged to fight for her by Valentine, backs down like a coward. *The Two Gentlemen of Verona*

THYREUS: A friend of Octavius Caesar. Octavius sends him to offer her anything she desires if she will leave Antony. Antony finds him kissing her hand and has him whipped. *Antony and Cleopatra*

TIMANDRA: One of Alcibiades' two mistresses. Timon curses her, encourages her to give men diseases, then gives her some treasure he has found, while still cursing her. *Timon of Athens*

TIME: He acts as a chorus at the start of Act IV to tell us that sixteen years have past, that Leontes is still repenting his follies and that his daughter, Perdita, is now a graceful girl. *The Winter's Tale*

TIMON: The hero of the play who starts as the most magnanimous of men, then, when he loses his fortunes and his so-called friends desert him, turns into the most spectacular misanthrope in drama.

His steward, Flavius, warns him he is being over-lavish, but Timon, a rich, noble Athenian, takes no notice, welcoming flatterers and fawners who crowd his house.

Generous to those in need, he does not listen to the cynical Apemantus who despises his naïve belief in the goodness of his friends. Suddenly, he is told by Flavius that he has lost all his property. One by one all his 'friends' refuse to loan him money, so he gives a final feast to which the vultures come, opens dishes which just contain warm water, hurls both water and dishes at the guests and drives them away. He goes to live in a cave where he discovers gold, giving it to anyone who passes. He gives some to the banished Alcibiades to help him devastate Athens and insults Apemantus and drives him away, though he gives thieves some gold as they are honest rogues. He beats a greedy poet and painter and refuses to help senators who urge him to help defeat Alcibiades. Only his servant Flavius escapes his wrath. He believes him the one honest man, but will not let him help him. Alcibiades takes Athens, but hears that the 'noble Timon' is dead.

Is the play satire, tragedy or both? Is Timon's extravagance the sign of his goodness or mere foolishness? Only a very fine actor can make the part a great one, can achieve the variety needed to make the scalding language not seem overblown after a time, and repetitious. *Timon of Athens*

TITANIA: Queen of the Fairies. She quarrels with Oberon, her King, because she will not give up a 'little changeling boy' to him. He puts her under a spell which makes her fall in love with the first thing that she sees—Bottom the Weaver, who has been given an ass's head by Puck. She has four fairies attend her weird beloved. Oberon later takes pity on her, releases her from the spell and is reconciled with her. *A Midsummer Night's Dream*

TITINIUS: A friend of Brutus and Cassius. The latter sends him to find out if some soldiers at Philippi are friend or foe. The brave Titinius finds they are Brutus's men, but Cassius thinks he has been captured and has Pindarus kill him. Titinius finds him dead, grieves that 'the sun of Rome is set', and kills himself after having put a garland on his friend's brow. *Julius Caesar*

TITUS ANDRONICUS: A Roman general and the tragic hero of the play that bears his name, a very popular Elizabethan horror-comic in its day, still viable as tragedy if skilfully enough performed.

Titus returns to Rome after conquering the Goths, bringing their Queen, Tamora, and three of her sons, as captives. His sons sacrifice the eldest of them. The people proclaim him Emperor, but he steps down in favour of Saturninus, who says he will marry his daughter Lavinia. Titus agrees. But Bassianus, Saturninus's brother, carries her off with the consent of Titus's sons. In a fight Titus kills his youngest son. Saturninus renounces Lavinia and marries Tamora, who now hates Titus and plans, with her Moorish lover, Aaron, to be revenged. Her sons, Chiron and Demetrius, kill Bassianus and rape and mutilate Lavinia, and two of Titus's sons are executed for the deed. Aaron tells Titus they will be spared if he gives his hand as ransom, but he gets it back with his sons' heads.

Crazed with despair, Titus finds out the truth and plots his revenge. He pretends to be mad, and with his remaining son leading a Gothic army on Rome, cuts the throats of Chiron and Demetrius while Lavinia holds a basin with her stumps to receive the blood. He bakes the boys in a pie and serves them to their mother, having first killed his dishonoured daughter. After Tamora has eaten her children, he kills her, upon which Saturninus kills him.

To bring reality to such extreme melodrama is not easy, especially as much, though not all, of the verse is below Shakespearean standards. Also Titus's endless misfortunes demand endless variety from the actor to make the rôle truly tragic and believable. *Titus Andronicus*

TOPAS, SIR: Feste the jester adopts this name when he pretends to be a curate to torment the imprisoned Malvolio. *Twelfth Night*

TOUCHSTONE: The clever Fool of Duke Frederick's Court. He accompanies Rosalind and Celia to the Forest of Arden and continues his career of puncturing pomposity and human foolishness. However, he himself courts a country girl, Audrey, whom he admits is 'an ill-favoured thing . . . but mine own'. He gets rid of her former sweetheart, the simple William, who is bemused by his flow of words. Some of these are obscure to modern audiences, but some, given the right actor, are still genuinely funny. He is a natural philosopher. *As You Like It*

TRANIO: Lucentio's servant. He pretends to be his master so that Lucentio can woo Bianca in disguise and put off other would-be suitors. He gets Baptista, Bianca's father, to consent to the match and forces a pedant to pretend to be Vincentio, Lucentio's father. When Lucentio's actual father arrives, he runs away. *The Taming of the Shrew*

TRAVERS: A retainer of Northumberland who tells him about the defeat of Hotspur at Shrewsbury. *2 Henry IV*

TREBONIUS: One of the conspirators. He agrees when Brutus insists that Antony shall not be killed as well as Caesar. He draws Antony to one side when the petition is presented to Caesar in the Senate. After the assassination, he says that Antony has 'Fled to his house amaz'd.' *Julius Caesar*

TRESSEL AND BERKELEY: Two attendants of Lady Anne. *Richard III*

TRINCULO: Alonso's jester. He comes upon the monster, Caliban, when drunk and they hide under Caliban's cloak in a storm where Stephano discovers them. He joins with Stephano in Caliban's plot to kill Prospero, but the spirit, Ariel, lands the three drunks in a slimy pool and sets spirits disguised as dogs on them. Failing in their plot, they are forgiven by Prospero. *The Tempest*

TROILUS: The romantic young hero of a very cynical play. He loves Cressida, daughter of Calchas, a priest, who has gone over to the Greeks. Her uncle, Pandarus, acts as a go-between. In an argument about whether or not Helen should be handed back and peace made, Troilus the romantic will not hear of it. The lovers later swear eternal fidelity, but Calchas has his daughter exchanged for Antenor, a captured Trojan. Troilus gives her a sleeve as a token of his love, but he is taken outside the walls of Troy by Ulysses and Thersites and watches his 'false Cressida' give the sleeve to Diomedes and embracing him. He fights his rival the next day but does not kill him. The play ends with Troilus shaken by Hector's death, and bitter and heartbroken at his loss.

Some believe Shakespeare's view of Troilus's love was ironic, in keeping with the play. It may well partly be, but surely not wholly. 'I am giddy, expectation whirls me round,' says Troilus before finally meeting her at the beginning of his most famous speech, which though it proves that Troilus is not innocent, is hardly ironic. *Troilus and Cressida*

TUBAL: A Jewish friend of Shylock who tells him that his daughter, Jessica, is spending his money and squandering his jewels in Genoa, but cheers him up by telling him that Antonio's ships are wrecked. *The Merchant of Venice*

TUTOR TO RUTLAND: He tries to prevent Clifford from killing the youth. Clifford spares the tutor because he is a priest. *3 Henry VI*

TYBALT: Juliet's 'spitfire' cousin. He wishes to attack Romeo when he spots him at the Capulets' ball, but Capulet stops him. Later, he picks a quarrel with him. Romeo will not fight the fiery, proud youth because he is related to Juliet, so Mercutio does and is killed. This stings Romeo into killing Tybalt. *Romeo and Juliet*

TYRREL, SIR JAMES. He is summoned by Richard and willingly agrees to kill the Princes in the Tower. He gets Dighton and Forrest to do the killing, confesses his horror of the deed in a soliloquy, then tells Richard he has seen them dead and buried. *Richard III*

U

ULYSSES: A Greek general. He believes that Greek morale has been weakened because the great Achilles has been skulking in his tent and laughing with Patroclus. In a famous speech on 'degree', he stresses the need for an ordered rule. He suggests making Achilles jealous by having Ajax accept a challenge from Hector, later praising the simple-minded Ajax and craftily telling Achilles that he is being overshadowed by the man of the moment— Ajax. With Thersites and Troilus, he watches Cressida prove false to Troilus with Diomedes, and does his best to comfort the youth. Achilles finally rouses himself for action thanks to Ulysses's scheming.

Ulysses seems the most sensible figure in the play, not so much the hero or villain of it as has been argued, but the man of stature in a world undermined by lesser men. *Troilus and Cressida*

URSULA: One of Hero's gentlewomen. She is in the scheme to make Beatrice love Benedick, talking about his merits to Hero when Beatrice is listening. She realizes that Beatrice has swallowed the bait. *Much Ado About Nothing*

URSWICK, SIR CHRISTOPHER: He is sent by Stanley (Derby) to tell Richmond that Stanley's son is being held as a hostage. *Richard III*

V

VALENTINE: A (silent) relative of Titus, who, when Titus seems mad, helps him shoot arrows with messages for the gods on them. *Titus Andronicus*

One of Orsino's gentlemen. He reports that he was not admitted to see Olivia and that she intends to mourn seven years for her brother. He tells Cesario (Viola in disguise) how much Orsino favours him. *Twelfth Night*

One of the two gentlemen of Verona, and by far the more likeable. He goes to Milan where he falls in love with Silvia, the Duke's daughter. His alleged friend Proteus, wanting her for himself, gets him banished by telling the Duke that Valentine means to elope with Silvia. He flees and becomes the elected captain of a band of outlaws who later capture Silvia, on her way to find him. Proteus rescues her and is about to rape her when Valentine appears. He wins Silvia, wins over her father, whose choice for her turns out to be a coward, and charitably forgives his friend. *The Two Gentlemen of Verona*

VALERIA: A friend of Coriolanus's wife, Virgilia. Inclined to chatter, she praises Virgilia's 'pretty boy', announces that Corioli is under siege and tries to get her to come out of the house. She is present when Virgilia and Volumnia plead with Coriolanus to spare Rome. *Coriolanus*

VARRIUS: A friend of Pompey. He tells him Antony is expected in Rome. *Antony and Cleopatra*

A (silent) friend of the Duke. *Measure for Measure*

VARRO: *see* Claudius

VARRO'S SERVANTS: They try and collect a debt from Timon after his downfall, but fail. *Timon of Athens*

VAUGHAN, SIR THOMAS: He is executed with Rivers and Grey at Pomfret. *Richard III*

VAUX, SIR NICHOLAS: He is given charge of Buckingham, who is to be executed. *Henry VIII*

VAUX, SIR WILLIAM: He tells Queen Margaret that Cardinal Beaufort is dying—and cursing. *2 Henry VI*

VENICE, DUKE OF: The judge who presides at Antonio's trial. A merciful man, he pardons Shylock, as long as he turns Christian, gives half his estate to Antonio, and pays the state a fine. *The Merchant of Venice*

He appoints Othello commander against the Turks and, when he has listened to his story, urges Desdemona's father to accept Othello as her husband. *Othello*

VENTIDIUS: One of Antony's generals. He defeats the Parthians, but does not pursue them in case Antony should become jealous. *Antony and Cleopatra*

Rescued by Timon from a debtors' prison, but when Timon needs money desperately, though Ventidius has inherited a fortune, he will not help. *Timon of Athens*

VERGES: A 'headborough' (petty constable). He is a partner of Dogberry and tells him that all their men are good and true. He is an old man who 'will be talking', according to Dogberry. He tells Leonato that Borachio and Conrade have been arrested and agrees with what Dogberry says at their trial. *Much Ado About Nothing*

VERNON: He plucks a white rose in the Temple Garden, so becoming a Yorkist. He quarrels with the Lancastrian Basset and asks the King if he may challenge him to single combat, but Henry refuses. *1 Henry VI*

VERNON, SIR RICHARD: He joins Hotspur's rebellion, making a speech about Hal on arrival at Shrewsbury in language worthy of Hotspur himself. In a council, he suggests caution, partly because the horses are exhausted. He and Worcester keep back the King's offer of peace from Hotspur. In the battle, Vernon is captured and executed. *1 Henry IV*

VINCENTIO: The Duke of Vienna. He has not been able to enforce his morality laws, so hands over his powers to Angelo, saying he is going to Poland. Actually, he disguises himself as Friar Lodowick and stays in Vienna to watch how

Angelo fares. The hypocritical, sensual Angelo offers to spare Claudio's life if his sister Isabella gives herself to him, so the Duke works out a scheme to save his life and her honour, telling Isabella to pretend to give in, then substituting Mariana, whom Angelo has deserted, in his bed. The Duke later reveals himself, pretending at first to disbelieve the girls' story. Then he makes Angelo marry Mariana, and Claudio the girl whom he originally seduced, and so got into the clutches of Angelo. The Duke himself says he loves Isabella. *Measure for Measure*

Lucentio's father. He meets Petruchio on his way from Pisa to Padua and hears that his son has married Bianca. When he arrives he finds a Pedant is impersonating him, and almost has him arrested. Fortunately, Lucentio arrives, tells him all and is forgiven. *The Taming of the Shrew*

VIOLA: Sebastian's twin sister. She is shipwrecked on the coast of Illyria, thinking that her brother is drowned. She disguises herself as a page, Cesario, and serves Duke Orsino. She at once falls in love with her master, who is himself pining for Olivia. She goes to woo her for him, manages to get admitted with difficulty, and meets Olivia, who complicates matters by falling in love with her.

Orsino sends her once again to Olivia after refusing to believe Viola that someone (herself) may be as much in love with him as he with Olivia, and, after meeting Feste, the jester, she finds herself being wooed by the infatuated Olivia. Sir Toby and his friends now persuade poor Sir Andrew Aguecheek, who has hopes of Olivia himself, to challenge Cesario.

Sir Andrew's letter is not up to standard, so Sir Toby challenges Viola for him. She says she is no fighter and the ensuing non-duel proves that neither of them are. It is interrupted by Sebastian's friend Antonio, who thinks that Viola is Sebastian. Antonio is arrested as an enemy of Orsino and asks Viola for money Sebastian borrowed from him: he is thunderstruck when Viola disclaims all knowledge of it. When she and the Duke go to Olivia's house, he accuses her of gross ingratitude. Then the dazed girl is confronted by Olivia who greets her as husband, she having married Sebastian. Now even the Duke calls her a dissembling cub, and to top everything, Sir Andrew accuses her of running him through. Fortunately, Sebastian appears and all is explained. Orsino prophesies that when he sees Cesario as a woman she will become Orsino's mistress and his fancy's Queen.

Viola is a devoted and loving character. *Twelfth Night*

VIOLENTA: A (silent) friend of Diana's mother, the Widow. *All's Well that Ends Well*

VIRGILIA: Coriolanus's quiet, faithful wife, who vows to stay at home until he returns from his war against the Volscians. When he comes back he hails her as 'My gracious silence'. With her mother-in-law, Volumnia, and her son, she later goes out to try and stop him attacking Rome, which has banished him. They succeed, though Volumnia does nearly all the talking. *Coriolanus*

VOLTIMAND: *see* Cornelius

VOLUMNIA: The hero's overpowering mother. She is vastly proud of her son, as she makes clear in her first scene with Virgilia, his wife. When he returns from the wars in triumph, he kneels to her before greeting Virgilia. She later advises him not to show the contempt they both feel for the plebians until he has been elected consul. She breaks down when he is banished, and when he returns at the head of an army to attack Rome, she goes to his tent with Virgilia and Coriolanus's son and is mainly instrumental in making him change his mind. *Coriolanus*

VOLUMNIUS: This old schoolfellow of Brutus refuses to hold the sword on which he wishes to kill himself after his defeat at Philippi. When he hears the enemy approaching, he flees. *Julius Caesar*

W

WART: One of Falstaff's conscripts. *2 Henry IV*

WARWICK, EARL OF: He cheers the King about the size
of the Northumberland rebellion, and later tells him that
Prince Hal's character is finer than he realizes. *2 Henry IV*.
With the King in France. *Henry V*. He plucks a white rose
in the Temple Garden, so becoming a Yorkist. He is one
of the nobles eager to have Joan of Arc burnt. *1 Henry VI*

The son-in-law of the above, known as the Kingmaker. He
and his father accuse Suffolk of killing Gloucester. He
becomes a Yorkist and fights at St. Albans. *2 Henry VI*. After
York is killed, he is victor at Towton, then sees to it that
York's son is crowned Edward IV. He goes to France to
arrange that Lady Bona becomes Edward's wife, but while
there learns that Edward has married Lady Grey. Warwick
changes sides, and joins Queen Margaret. He captures
Edward and, having stripped him of his crown, returns it to
Henry VI. At Barnet he is killed. *3 Henry VI*
See also Plantagenet, Lady Margaret

WESTMORELAND, EARL OF: A supporter of the King
against Hotspur at Shrewsbury. *1 Henry IV*. He urges the
rebels, Mowbray, Hastings and the Archbishop of York to
make peace, then supports Prince John of Lancaster in his
despicable scheme to make them dismiss their army, after
which they are arrested for treason and executed. *2 Henry IV*.
His wish before Agincourt for 10,000 of those men not
working that day in England, sparks off Henry's St.
Crispin's Day speech. *Henry V*

Grandson of the above, and a Lancastrian who is furious
when the King makes York his heir. *3 Henry VI*

WHITEMORE, WALTER: A pirate. He loses an eye capturing
Suffolk. Later he beheads him. *2 Henry VI*

WIDOW: A widow of Florence and the mother of Diana whom Bertram plans to seduce. The widow lodges Helena, Bertram's abandoned wife, who promises her gold and a good dowry for her daughter if she will help her in a scheme for winning back Bertram by substituting herself in Diana's bed. The widow agrees. *All's Well that Ends Well*

Hortensio marries this 'lusty widow' after he has failed to win Bianca. *The Taming of the Shrew*

WILLIAM: A peasant in love with Audrey. Touchstone, the worldly jester, moves in and tells poor William to shun her or he will kill him in 150 different ways. With a 'God rest you merry, sir,' William departs. *As You Like It*

WILLIAMS, MICHAEL: An English soldier at Agincourt. The night before the battle he quarrels with the disguised Henry and exchanges gloves with him, saying he will box his ears after the battle. The King gives the glove to Fluellen, whom Williams attacks. Fluellen has him arrested, but Henry explains the truth and orders Williams to be given a gloveful of crowns. *Henry V*

WILLOUGHBY, LORD: Won over to Bolingbroke after the King confiscates John of Gaunt's lands and so deprives his son, Bolingbroke, of his inheritance. *Richard II*

WINCHESTER, BISHOPS OF: *see* Beaufort, Henry, *also* Gardiner

WITCHES: The three 'midnight hags' who hail Macbeth as Thane of Glamis, Thane of Cawdor and King hereafter. They hail his companion Banquo as a man who will beget kings. Later the 'weird sister' produces three Apparitions for Macbeth which seem to spell safety to him, but actually signify his downfall and death. They greatly influence Macbeth's actions and ambitions. *Macbeth*

WOODVILLE: The Lieutenant of the Tower. Acting on the Cardinal of Winchester's orders, he refuses to allow Gloucester and his men into the Tower. *1 Henry VI*

WORCESTER, THOMAS PERCY, EARL OF: He, his brother Northumberland, and his nephew Hotspur have an angry scene with Henry IV, whom Worcester reminds that he was put on the throne by the Percys. Resenting Henry's treatment of them, they plan to rebel. Worcester tries to calm the fiery Hotspur and later at Bangor, criticizes his impetuous exchanges with Glendower.

At Shrewsbury, before the battle, Worcester is offered a pardon by Henry for himself and his fellow rebels, but does not pass on the message, telling Vernon who is with him that the King will never keep his word. He then lies to Hotspur, claiming that Henry has abused him. He is captured and, for his failure to carry the message, is executed. A devious, dangerous character, utterly unlike his nephew. *1 Henry IV*

Y

YORICK: The dead court jester, a 'fellow of infinite jest', over whose skull Hamlet muses on life and death to Horatio. *Hamlet*

YORK, DUCHESS OF: Her husband decides that he must tell Henry Bolingbroke of their son, Aumerle's, treason. She begs her son to confess to Henry, then hastens to Windsor to the new King. With Henry helping her to get off her knees, she successfully pleads for her son. This 'frantic woman', as York calls her, is, despite her plight, comic relief. *Richard II*

The mother of Edward IV, Richard and Clarence. With her grandchildren she laments the death of Clarence, then hears from Queen Elizabeth of Edward's death. Later she curses her son, Richard, wishing she had strangled him in her womb. She calls him a toad and tells him, 'Bloody thou art, bloody will be thy end.' *Richard III*

YORK, EDMUND OF LANGLEY, DUKE OF: Richard's elderly uncle who vainly tries to prevent the growing rift between him and his other nephew Bolingbroke. He ineffectually attempts to be on both sides in a number of scenes, though from the moment he meets the returning Bolingbroke in Gloucestershire he, in effect, becomes his man. When his son Aumerle plots to murder Bolingbroke, now Henry IV, he wants him condemned, and reports the crime to Henry, but his Duchess saves their son by her frantic pleas. *Richard II*

YORK, DUKE OF: *see* Aumerle

YORK, RICHARD SCROOP, ARCHBISHOP OF: *see* Scroop

YORK, RICHARD, DUKE OF: As Richard Plantagenet, he quarrels with the Lancastrian Somerset and plucks a white rose in the Temple Garden, Somerset plucking a red one. Henry makes him Duke of York and he later fights in France under Talbot and is one of those who ferociously condemn Joan of Arc. *1 Henry VI*
He soliloquizes about how he will make Henry yield the crown, but Beaufort and Suffolk engineer his removal to suppress a revolt in Ireland. He returns determined to break Somerset's power, and unscrupulously triggers off the Wars of the Roses, defeating Henry and Queen Margaret at St. Albans where he kills Clifford. *2 Henry VI*
He agrees to peace if Henry makes him his heir, but, urged by his sons, Richard and Edward, sets out to grab the crown. He is captured at Wakefield, crowned with a paper crown by the 'she-wolf' Margaret, whom he memorably abuses, then is stabbed to death by her and young Clifford. York is a vividly drawn portrait of a cunning, brave and ambitious medieval baron. *3 Henry VI*

Edward IV's younger son, sent to the Tower with his brother, Edward, by Richard and later murdered there. In his scene with Richard he holds his own wittily against his wicked uncle, too wittily to amuse Richard at one point when the boy mocks his appearance. *Richard III*

The Characters — Play by Play

All's Well that Ends Well

	Act and Scene		Act and Scene
Bertram	I–I	Lavache	I–3
Clown	I–3	Mariana	III–5
Countess of Rousillon	I–I	Old Widow of Florence	III–5
Diana	III–5	Page	I–I
Duke of Florence	III–I	Parolles	I–I
Helena	I–I	Steward (Rinaldo)	I–3
King of France	I–2	Violenta	III–5
Lafeu	I–I		

Antony and Cleopatra

	Act and Scene		Act and Scene
Agrippa	II–2	Mark Antony	I–I
Alexas	I–2	Mecaenas	II–2
Canidius	III–7	Menas	II–I
Charmian	I–2	Menecrates	II–I
Cleopatra	I–I	Octavia	II–3
Clown	V–2	Octavius Caesar	I–4
Demetrius	I–I	Philo	I–I
Dercetas	IV–I2	Pompey (Sextus Pompeius)	II–I
Diomedes	IV–I2	Proculeius	V–I
Dolabella	III–I0	Scarus	III–8
Enobarbus	I–2	Seleucus	V–2
Eros	III–9	Silius	III–I
Euphronius	III–I0	Soothsayer	I–2
Gallus	V–I	Taurus	III–8
Iras	I–2	Thyreus	III–I0
Marcus Aemilius Lepidus	I–4	Varrius	II–I
Mardian	I–5	Ventidius	II–2

177

178

Hamlet

	Act and Scene		Act and Scene
Bernardo	I–I	Laertes	I–2
Claudius	I–2	Marcellus	I–I
Cornelius	I–2	Ophelia	I–3
Francisco	I–I	Osric	V–2
Fortinbras	IV–4	Players	II–2
Gertrude	I–2	Polonius	I–2
Ghost of Hamlet's father	I–I	Priest	V–I
Gravediggers	V–I	Reynaldo	II–I
Guildenstern	II–2	Rosencrantz	II–2
Hamlet	I–2	Voltimand	I–2
Horatio	I–I		

Henry IV, Part 1

	Act and Scene		Act and Scene
Bardolph	II–2	Michael, Sir	IV–4
Blunt, Sir Walter	I–3	Mistress Quickly	II–4
Chamberlain	II–I	Mortimer, Edmund	III–I
Douglas, Earl of	IV–I	Mortimer, Lady	III–I
Falstaff, Sir John	I–2	Northumberland, Earl of	I–3
Francis	II–4	Percy, Lady	II–3
Gadshill	II–I	Peto	II–2
Glendower, Owen	III–I	Poins	I–2
Henry IV, King	I–I	Scroop, Richard,	
Henry, Prince of Wales		Archbishop of York	IV–4
(Hal)	I–2	Vernon, Sir Richard	IV–I
Hotspur (Henry Percy)	I–3	Westmoreland, Earl of	I–I
Lancaster, John of	V–I	Worcester, Earl of	I–3

Henry IV, Part 2

	Act and Scene		Act and Scene
Bardolph	II–I	Gloucester, Humphrey of	IV–4
Bardolph, Lord	I–I	Gower	II–I
Blunt	IV–3	Harcourt	IV–4
Clarence, Thomas, Duke of	IV–4	Hastings, Lord	I–3
Colevile, Sir John	IV–3	Henry IV, King	III–I
Dancer	Epilogue	Henry, Prince of Wales	
Davy	V–I	(Prince Hal), later	
Doll Tearsheet	II–4	Henry V	II–2
Falstaff, Sir John	I–2	Lancaster, John of	IV–2
Fang and Snare	II–I	Lord Chief Justice	I–2

Henry IV, Part 2 (cont.)

Henry V

Henry VI, Part 1

Henry VI, Part 1 (cont.)

Henry VI, Part 2

Henry VI, Part 3

Henry VIII

Julius Caesar

	Act and Scene		Act and Scene
Aemilius Lepidus	III–1	Lucius	II–1
Artemidorus	II–3	Marcus Brutus	I–2
Calphurnia	I–2	Mark Antony	I–2
Casca	I–2	Messala	IV–3
Cassius	I–2	Metellus Cimber	II–1
Cicero	I–2	Octavius Caesar	IV–1
Cinna	I–3	Pindarus	V–3
Cinna, a poet	III–3	Popilius Lena	III–1
Clitus	V–5	Portia	I–2
Dardanius	V–5	Publius	II–2
Decius Brutus	I–2	Soothsayer	I–2
Flavius and Marullus	I–1	Strato	V–3
Julius Caesar	I–2	Trebonius	II–1
Ligarius	II–1	Varro and Claudius	IV–3
Lucilius and Titinius	IV–2	Young Cato and Volumnius	V–3

King Lear

	Act and Scene		Act and Scene
Albany, Duke of	I–1	France, King of	I–1
Burgundy, Duke of	I–1	Gloucester, Earl of	I–1
Cordelia	I–1	Goneril	I–1
Cornwall, Duke of	I–1	Kent, Earl of	I–1
Curan	II–1	Lear, King	I–1
Doctor	IV–4	Old Man	IV–1
Edgar	I–2	Oswald	I–3
Edmund	I–1	Regan	I–1
Fool	I–4		

King John

	Act and Scene		Act and Scene
Arthur, Duke of Britaine	II–1	Henry, Prince	V–7
Blanch	II–1	John, King	I–1
Bigot, Lord	V–2	Lewis the Dauphin	II–1
Burgh, Hubert de	III–3	Lymoges, Duke of Austria	II–1
Chatillon	I–1	Melun	V–2
Constance	II–1	Pandulph, Cardinal	III–1
Elinor, Queen	I–1	Pembroke, Earl of	I–1
Essex, Earl of	I–1	Peter of Pomfret	IV–2
Faulconbridge, Lady	I–1	Philip, King of France	II–1
Faulconbridge, Robert	I–1	Philip the Bastard	I–1
Gurney, James	I–1	Salisbury, Earl of	I–1

Love's Labour's Lost

	Act and Scene		Act and Scene
Armado, Don Adriano de	I–2	Katharine	II–I
Berowne	I–I	Longaville	I–I
Boyet	II–I	Maria	II–I
Costard	I–I	Mercade	V–2
Dull	I–I	Moth	I–2
Dumain	I–I	Nathaniel, Sir	IV–2
Ferdinand, King of Navarre	I–I	Princess of France	II I
Holofernes	IV–2	Rosaline	II–I
Jaquenetta	I–2		

Macbeth

	Act and Scene		Act and Scene
Angus	I–3	Macbeth	I–3
Banquo	I 9	Macduff	I–6
Boy, Macduff's son	IV–2	Malcolm	I–2
Caithness	V–4	Menteith	V–4
Donalbain	I–2	Porter	II–3
Duncan, King of Scotland	I–2	Ross	I–2
English Doctor	IV–3	Scotch Doctor	V–I
Fleance	II–I	Sergeant	I–2
Hecate	III–5	Seyton	V–3
Lady Macbeth	I–5	Siward	V–4
Lady Macduff	IV–2	Three Witches	I–I
Lennox	I–2	Young Siward	V–4

Measure for Measure

	Act and Scene		Act and Scene
Abhorson	IV–2	Froth	II–I
Angelo	I–I	Isabella	I–4
Barnardine	IV–3	Juliet	I–2
Claudio	I–2	Lucio	I–2
Duke Vincentio	I–I	Mariana	IV–I
Elbow	II–I	Mistress Overdone	I–2
Escalus	I–I	Pompey Bum	I–2
Francisca	I–4	Provost	I–2
Friar Peter	IV–5	Varrius	IV–5
Friar Thomas	I–3		

The Merchant of Venice

The Merry Wives of Windsor

A Midsummer Night's Dream

Much Ado About Nothing

Othello

Pericles

Richard II

Richard II (cont.)

	Act and Scene		Act and Scene
Fitzwater, Lord	IV–I	Queen to King Richard	II–2
Gardener	III–4	Richard II, King	I–I
Gaunt, John of, Duke of		Ross, Lord	II–I
Lancaster	I–I	Salisbury, Earl of	II–4
Gloucester, Duchess of	I–2	Scroop, Sir Stephen	III–2
Hotspur (Henry Percy)	II–3	Surrey, Duke of	IV–I
Mowbray, Thomas, Duke		Westminster, Abbot of	IV–I
of Norfolk	I–I	Willoughby, Lord	II–I
Northumberland, Earl of	II–I	York, Duchess of	V–2
Pierce of Exton, Sir	V–4	York, Edmund, Duke of	II–I

Richard III

	Act and Scene		Act and Scene
Anne, Lady	I–2	Margaret	I–3
Blount, Sir James	V–2	Margaret Plantagenet, Lady	II–2
Brakenbury, Sir Robert	I–I	Murderers	I–3
Brandon, Sir William	V–3	Norfolk, Duke of	V–3
Buckingham, Duke of	I–3	Oxford, Earl of	V–2
Canterbury, Archbishop of,		Queen Elizabeth	I–3
Cardinal Bourchier	III–I	Ratcliff, Sir Richard	II–2
Catesby, Sir William	I–3	Richmond, Henry of,	
Clarence, George, Duke of	I–I	later Henry VII	V–2
Dorset, Marquess of, and		Rivers, Earl	I–3
Lord Grey	I–3	Stanley, Lord (Derby)	I–3
Edward IV, King	II–I	Surrey, Earl of	V–3
Edward, Prince of Wales,		Tressel and Berkeley	I–2
later Edward V	III–I	Tyrrel, Sir James	IV–2
Ely, John Morton, Bishop		Urswick, Christopher	IV–5
of	III–4	Vaughan, Sir Thomas	III–3
Gloucester, Richard, Duke		York, Archbishop of,	
of, later Richard III	I–I	Thomas Rotheram	II–4
Hastings, Lord	I–I	York, Duchess of	II–2
Herbert, Sir Walter	V–2	York, Richard, Duke of	II–4
Lord Mayor of London	III–I	York son of Clarence	II–2
Lovel, Lord	III–4		

Romeo and Juliet

	Act and Scene		Act and Scene
Abraham	I–I	Benvolio	I–I
Apothecary	V–I	Capulet	I–I
Balthasar	I–I	Chorus	Prologue

Romeo and Juliet (cont.)

	Act and Scene		Act and Scene
Escalus, Prince of Verona	I–1	Montague	I–1
Friar Laurence	II–3	Nurse	I–3
Friar John	V–2	Paris	I–2
Gregory	I–1	Peter	II–4
Juliet	I–3	Romeo	I–1
Lady Capulet	I–1	Sampson	I–1
Lady Montague	I–1	Tybalt	I–1
Mercutio	I–4		

The Taming of the Shrew

	Act and Scene		Act and Scene
Baptista	I–1	Lord	Induction 1
Bianca	I–1	Lucentio	I–1
Biondello	I–1	Page	Induction 2
Curtis	IV–1	Pedant	IV–2
Gremio	I–1	Petruchio	I–2
Grumio	I–2	Sly, Christopher	Induction 1
Hortensio	I–1	Tranio	I–1
Hostess, Huntsmen,		Vincentio	IV–5
Players, Servants	Induction 1	Widow	V–2
Katharina	I–1		

The Tempest

	Act and Scene		Act and Scene
Adrian	II–1	Iris, Ceres, Juno	IV–1
Alonso, King of Naples	I–1	Master of a Ship,	
Antonio	I–1	Boatswain, Mariners	I–1
Ariel	I–2	Miranda	I–2
Caliban	I–2	Prospero	I–2
Ferdinand	I–1	Sebastian	I–1
Francisco	II–1	Stephano	II–2
Gonzalo	I–1	Trinculo	II–2

Timon of Athens

	Act and Scene		Act and Scene
Alcibiades	I–1	Hortensius	III–4
Apemantus	I–1	Lucilius	I–1
Caphis	II–1	Lucius	III–2
Flaminius	II–2	Lucullus	III–1
Flavius	I–2	Old Athenian	I–1

Timon of Athens (cont.)

Titus Andronicus

Troilus and Cressida

Twelfth Night

Twelfth Night (cont.)

The Two Gentlemen of Verona

The Winter's Tale